I have known Dr. Maureen for over twenty years, and it has been an honor. She is purposeful and intentional about every aspect of her life and exercises discipline to accomplish her loftiest goals. It is through her coaching that she is effective in getting others to see their talent and unique abilities and inspire them to greater success. It is an honor and a blessing to know her.
Rev. Dr. Adriene B. Wright, Founder, President, and CEO of Abelita, LLC

Rev. Dr. Maureen is a mighty woman of God who "Lives Her Life from the Inside Out." I am humbled and privileged to have been under her divine coaching for the past three years learning tools, principles, and strategies needed to shift my life into alignment with the "Divine Coach" (The Holy Spirit). Over the course of these past 3 years, her coaching has taught me to be more resilient; and more purposeful in where God is leading me.
Dr. Brenda Jarmon, Sowing Seeds of Faith, Inc.

Dr Maureen is one of those rare individuals that the more you know them the more you like them. Her extraordinary life has provided so much hard-earned wisdom that gives great depth to her perspective on life. I have had the pleasure of teaching alongside her and watched how she inspires and impacts everyone around her.
Roddy Galbraith, SpeakerPro

I consider it an absolute pleasure to have Dr. Maureen as my leadership coach, spiritual advisor, and personal friend. I have witnessed Dr. Maureen's perseverance, faithfulness, and love for the Lord, her church, family, and community. She is using her God-given talents, skills, and abilities to influence and impact the ministry, community, and marketplace for the glory of God.
Dwight Owens, CEO of Financial Fitness Group, LLC

Dr. Maureen's soft-spoken demeanor and elegant speaking style creates a captivating presence, while her awesome personality and thoughtful coaching approach makes her a truly transformative mentor. Working with her is an enriching experience that leaves a lasting impact on personal growth and empowers individuals to achieve their goals with confidence.
Jackie John, CEO & Founder, New Version Coaching & Consulting

Dr Maureen McIntosh Alberts is a true beacon of light and empowerment for women all over the world. Her dedication to uplifting and guiding women through her roles as pastor, author, and coach is nothing short of inspiring. In her book, she shares profound insights and wisdom that will transform lives. This book is a must read for anyone seeking guidance, inspiration, and a path to personal and spiritual growth.
Nancy Alert, Associate Broker

Maureen has proven herself to be an outstanding Transformational Coach. This outstanding capability is driven and informed by her ability to connect, impact and influence as she helps others make the required changes in their lives to become the best version of themselves.
Keston Nancoo, CEO of Guardian Group

Transforming Pain into Purpose

Transforming Pain into Purpose

15 Personal Stories of Resilience, Hope, and Renewal

Dr. Maureen McIntosh-Alberts

Transforming Pain into Purpose
15 Personal Stories of Resilience, Hope, and Renewal

Copyright © 2023 Dr. Maureen McIntosh-Alberts

ISBN: 979-8-218-27789-5

Published by McIntosh Publishers, LLC

All rights reserved. No part of this book may be reproduced or transmitted in any form or by any means, electronic or mechanical, including photocopying and recording, or by an information storage and retrieval system, without permission in writing from the author.

DEDICATION

To my esteemed co-authors,

This anthology, Transforming Pain into Purpose, stands as a testament to the power of collaboration and the resilience of the human spirit. Each of you has poured your heart and soul into crafting a chapter that not only shares your personal journey but also offers a beacon of hope to all who read it.

In the pages of this book, we have collectively woven a tapestry of experiences, wisdom, and inspiration. Through your words, you have illuminated the path from despair to determination, from adversity to achievement, and from pain to purpose. Your dedication, passion, and unwavering commitment to turning life's challenges into opportunities for growth and transformation have not only enriched this anthology but have touched the lives of countless readers who will find solace and inspiration within these pages.

As co-authors, you have brought your unique perspectives, voices, and stories to this collaborative effort. Together, we have created a literary mosaic that reflects the beauty that can emerge from the darkest of times.

I want to express my deepest gratitude for the trust you placed in this project and for the dedication you showed in sharing your personal stories. It is an honor and a privilege to stand alongside such talented and resilient individuals.

May our collective words serve as a source of inspiration, encouragement, and empowerment.

FOREWORD

In life, we are often faced with challenges that test the very core of our being, leaving us with pain, both mental and physical, that seems insurmountable. Yet, it is in these moments of adversity that the true potential for transformation lies. "Transforming Pain into Purpose" is an anthology that weaves a tapestry of life, delving deep into the power of turning anguish into an opportunity for growth, resilience, and, ultimately, purpose.

In my own journey over seven decades, I have met so many beautiful women whose stories tear your hearts to shred, yet with glory and grace, these brave women have overcome the odds and become beacons of light. Their indomitable spirit and unwavering strength have inspired me beyond measure. And in this anthology, they generously share those tears and joys that make us real human beings, connecting us on a profound level of empathy and understanding.

One such beautiful woman is Dr Maureen McIntosh-Alberts, creator of this anthology of deeply moving stories from fifteen brave and courageous women. Her own message has made a huge imprint on my life, and I share it here.

Remember, you are not alone on your journey. The same power that breathed life into the universe resides within you. Draw strength from the love and support of those around you and seek solace in the presence of a God who walks beside you every step of the way.

Within the pages of this collection, you will embark on a journey guided by remarkable writers who have traversed the turbulent seas of suffering and emerged on the shores of purposeful living. Each thread in this rich tapestry explores unique themes on how the burdens of mental or physical ailments can be alchemized into a force of positive change.

The themes lay the foundation for our expedition by demonstrating the profound impact that pain can have on reshaping the trajectory of our lives. Through personal stories and introspective reflections, these writers share how they have harnessed the transformative potential of their suffering, weaving it into the fabric of their existence, creating patterns of newfound meaning and purpose.

You are invited to think critically and understand the issues of your lives. There are stories to question the nature of our afflictions and to delve into the depths of understanding their origins and implications. By adopting a critical mindset, we are empowered to confront our challenges with clarity and insight, weaving threads of wisdom that turn our pain into a catalyst for growth rather than an anchor weighing us down.

You will find you are asked questions to challenge your choices and urged to take an active role in your healing journey. By seeking knowledge, exploring alternative approaches, and challenging the status quo, we interlace threads of curiosity and empowerment, opening ourselves to a world of possibilities, discovering the path that aligns with our authentic selves.

We find stories that help you take action. You, the reader, will find yourself somewhere in each chapter. As women, we are reminded that our choices weave the tapestry of transformation. Armed with newfound awareness, we learn to make intentional decisions that will positively impact our lives, whether it involves seeking alternative medical opinions, adopting healthier lifestyles, or embracing holistic healing practices.

The anthology leads by example to instruct us to "take charge of your life and DO what is necessary," where the writers become master weavers, creating intricate patterns of hope and resilience. Each chapter shares triumphs, unveiling the spiritual and material dimensions of each journey. These courageous souls exhibit the power of taking charge of one's life, demonstrating that purpose is not merely discovered but actively woven into the fabric of existence.

As you journey through the profound narratives in "Transforming Pain into Purpose," you may find solace and wisdom within the woven threads of others. Each story will offer a guiding light, illuminating the path towards purpose, and revealing the boundless strength that resides within all of us. May this anthology serve as a beautifully crafted tapestry of inspiration and empowerment, reminding you that, no matter how intricate the pattern of pain, you have the power to transform it into purpose. Embrace your journey for within it lies the key to unlocking the fullness of your being.

In unity and resilience, women rise to shine their light together. I am so grateful to introduce this book to you.

Dr Pauline Crawford
Chief Vision Officer, Corporate Heart International

Author of *The Power of Authentic Harmony – Magical Conversations That Transform Our World*

Contents

DEDICATION 7

FOREWORD 8

Chapter 1: The Journey to Wholeness is Not Painless but Get There Anyhow.. 13
By Dr. Mary Edosomwan

Chapter 2: Surrender: Broken for Sweetness & Purpose 23
By Valerie O' Gorman

Chapter 3: Follow the Money: Diary of a Patient, Her Doctors, and Big Pharma 31
By Ann LeMaster

Chapter 4: The Power of Forgiveness. 39
By Dr. Carmia Hines

Chapter 5: The Handing Over of a Diamond 48
By Cindy-Ann Lewis

Chapter 6: The Entrapment of Fear into the Realization of Purpose 56
By Patricia Juba

Chapter 7: Overcoming Pain in the Workplace: Aptitude, Attitude, Altitude... 64
By Maria Veronica Rodrigues

Chapter 8: Overcoming Life's Twist and Turns 70
By Novellette Edwards

Chapter 9: A Purpose in Pain 76
By Rania Soliman

Chapter 10: The Final Run 85
By Mavis H. Bubb

Chapter 11: Finding Understanding While Persevering Through Pain 93
By Dr. Catherine Pearson

Chapter 12: The Power of Anchoring on Faith, Truth, Passion, and Purpose 102
By Ilka V. Wilson

Chapter 13: When Life Hands You Lemons 111
By Dawn Kirk

Chapter 14: Living Beyond Loss: Embracing Resilience and Finding Purpose... 120
By Nicky Cuesta

Chapter 15: Finding Life After Death.. 129
By Dr. Maureen McIntosh-Alberts

Chapter 1:
The Journey to Wholeness is Not Painless but Get There Anyhow
By Dr. Mary Edosomwan

"Every experience that you have and will have upon the Earth encourages the alignment of your personality with your soul. Every circumstance and situation gives you the opportunity to choose this path, to allow your soul to shine through you, to bring into the physical world through you its unending and unfathomable reverence for and love of Life." — Gary Zukav,

It's been approximately twelve years since my only son, my best friend and confidante departed for heaven without saying goodbye. My heart was broken into too many pieces to count. I felt blood flowing from my heart into my stomach in total disbelief and shock. Suddenly, I am awakened to the reality of my loss as the connection between the spirit, soul, and body is disconnected. I remember saying to myself repeatedly "So it is true? My only son is gone?" Grief like an avalanche rapidly overtook my soul and overwhelmed my spirit. My body was weighed down, and I collapsed to the floor in uncontrollable tears. No matter what I tried, I couldn't get out of bed, the spirit was willing, but the body was too immobile to act. Thinking only of the physical anomaly, I called the doctor, who prescribed antidepressant medication. I made a conscious decision not to take the antidepressant.

Growing up we were taught to put a bandage on physical wounds. Unfortunately, for emotional and soul woundedness, we were told not to cry, deal with it, shut up, and keep it moving. Growing up, in most Christian homes, you were told to pray about it and give all your troubles to Jesus, and at the church, you are told to leave all your troubles at the altar. But no one cared to explain the process of spiritual surrender and how to manage the emotional triggers. So, from generation to generation, we raised children who hid their anxiety, sorrows, shame, suicidal tendencies, and disappointments. By the time we reach adulthood, we have mastered the art of covering up emotional baggage with a gigantic bandage of activities and accomplishments.

So, there I was, as first lady of a church, Sunday school and Bible study teacher, and intercessory prayer leader, but my child is dead, yet I was not equipped with bereavement management. I couldn't ask God why He allowed my son to depart this world before me. The answer to the "why question" (Theodicy) belongs to God for He sees and knows all things: "For his eyes are on the ways of a man, and he sees all his steps," (Job 34:21). But my questions to God were: how I can go on living? How can I ever overcome the shame and failure as a mother interceding for other children who recovered or delivered, yet mine died? The combination of humiliation and defeat drove me to my knees day and night as I sought the Lord.

Transformative Encounter:

Then one night, I had a supernatural encounter where I was taken to another realm. By encounter, I mean the process of transformation or a supernatural experience that brings the reality of God to a person. I was invited into a dwelling place, but the gate entrance was extremely narrow for me to enter. An "angel" or celestial being (I would call him) was wearing fully protected armor; and came to my aid by rotating the gate to allow for my entrance into the dwelling place. He proceeded to teach me the art of Fencing with a very long, heavy sword, being gentle with me as I had no protective garment for such a fight. I was directed to a building with a long hallway. As I walked along the hallway, to my right was a big dining hall with long tables and people sitting on both sides of the table. Towards the end of the table was my son wearing gray sweatpants and a hooded top. He was very happy, enjoying the conversation at the end of their meal. Being the gentleman he was, he began to clear his plates from the dining table. My heart was flooded with joy and happy tears began to roll down both eyes. This supernatural encounter opened the door to many conversations and instructions regarding the next course of action for my life.

Destiny Redefined.

Among these dialogues were the instructions to go back to my son's school and finish what he started. Little did I know that God was redefining and redirecting the purpose of my life. Like a rag doll, broken, battered, and missing a leg; I did as commanded. Confronting the site of the death of your loved one is most difficult, yet necessary for inner transformation and healing.

For the first three years, I traveled approximately two to three hours one way from Fairfax to Richmond, VA every Friday & Saturday to complete graduate studies and earned a master's degree in Divinity for my son. Furthermore, on my first night, additional instruction came for me to complete a Doctor of Ministry in Grief and Bereavement Management in a school that didn't offer any course in that discipline. I kept the second vision to myself for fear of anyone calling me crazy. Through the divine grace of God and supernatural providence, "Grief and Loss: Death and Dying" education came to the campus of Virginia Union University just before I completed the Master of Divinity. The transition to the doctoral degree was green-lighted by the vision of God being fulfilled before my eyes.

Apostle Paul said it best, "And my God shall supply all your need according to His riches in glory by Christ Jesus," (Philippians 4:19).

You will find the compelling story of how God gave me a reason to live through the death cry to wholeness in my first book: *Broken Hearted: A Mother's Journey to Wholeness*. In my human mind, I was developing a theological grief model for spiritual healing (Death Cry to Wholeness), but God was healing my grief while gifting a unique spiritual pathway to wholeness to the world at large. You can find complete information at the Center for Grief and Wholeness.com.

In this chapter, I would like to challenge everyone to never give up on God in their journey to wholeness. The task may seem daunting, but it is designed so you do not rely on yourself: "For my thoughts are not your thoughts, neither are your ways my ways, saith the LORD. For as the heavens are higher than the earth, so are my ways higher than your ways, and my thoughts than your thoughts" (Isaiah 55:8-9).

What is wholeness?

Wholeness is a state of being in which we experience a deep sense of harmony and equilibrium in all areas of our lives including the physical, emotional, mental, and spiritual. While the journey to wholeness is not painless get there anyhow by allowing the Holy Spirit to lead and guide you.

Soul, Spirit, and Body

The soul is made in the image of God, the most valuable, priceless material not humanly quantifiable. The human soul is more valuable than all the riches of this world. The soul houses the Mind to think, the Will to decide and the Heart to feel. It is where our emotions are stored including emotional baggage. Coded within our soul is the power of resilience, which allows for rebounding from challenges: the Bible says: "The godly may trip seven times, but they will get up again. But one disaster is enough to overthrow the wicked," (Proverb 24:16). The soul is also the site of compassion, responsible for our ability to experience joy, love, and other emotions such as grief. The soul is the seat of our emotions and thoughts with a distinctive personality, reflecting our unique individuality, distinct likes, dislikes, and quirks. Avoiding prolonged suffering requires healing intervention within your soul.

The spirit is the part of us that connects with God and God resides and dwells there. God's intention and divine purpose flow out from this dwelling place. Thus, being whole in spirit means that we experience and accomplish all that God has designed for us but doing so while residing in a place of perfect peace, unspeakable joy with full liberty, and without hindrances.

The body is the physical aspect of our being, the tangible vessel that houses the soul and spirit. The body is mortal and subject to decay and will eventually die, unlike the spirit and soul. The body also gets sick when the soul is sick. As stated in 1 John 3:3 "Beloved, I wish above all things that you prosper and be in good health even as your soul prospers."

Soul Rebirth:

The purpose of sharing the various human components is to ensure that self-care is inclusive of all. As we plunge deeper into depression and complicated grief, the focus should be more on healing the soul and spirit than the body. The soul is the site mostly involved with the pain of death especially if you truly loved the departed soul. To the extent that you love, the greater the intensity of your agony and mourning. Love and pain occupy both sides of the same coin, they are inseparable.

Of the many diseases affecting the soul, hopelessness is the deadliest, for a soul without hope is dead. Every building block of your being will fall apart. You will feel confused, bewildered, angry, desperate, helpless, and hopeless. But this is the time your Soul is undergoing a makeover. Your old self is being stripped away and the new you are emerging like a butterfly out of a cocoon.

Learning to Surrender

Learning to surrender all worries and cares to God requires that you go inward to commune with your soul. King David said in a conversation with his soul "Why are you downcast, O my soul? Why so disturbed within me? Put your hope in God, for I will yet praise him, my Savior, and my God" (Psalm 43:5). The Bible is full of men and women who had encounters with God, and we see from scripture the corresponding exploits that validated those encounters. The scripture declares that "...the people who know their God will display strength and take action," (Daniel 11:32). This is a great promise to everyone going through grief and other mayhem – provided you seek to know the God within you. God almighty is revealing Himself to His sons and daughters through different dimensions of Himself so that we can learn from Him progressively, on our way to wholeness (becoming one with God).

I experienced a paradigm shift that significantly altered my trajectory when Naomi from the book of Ruth came alive to assist and walk along my journey to wholeness. Your walk with God and your faith journey are directly proportional to the experience that you have with God, and your exploits are dependent on your encounters as you seek and surrender to God. It was as though Naomi became my mentor, assisting me from her experience with grief and bitterness. God had a harvest awaiting her in her journey to wholeness- so it shall be for all who accept the journey to go back to God.

Lessons from the Journey to Wholeness

Finally, achieving wholeness after life's challenges requires a commitment to both personal and spiritual growth, and so is the willingness to lean on the Godhead and community for support. Below are some suggestions for the bereaved and supporters from both personal and professional experiences. Bear in mind that the grief journey is different for everyone:

1. Develop a support system.

Surrounding yourself with supportive people who can provide encouragement can be an effective healing process. God required that grief be a communal activity. The wailing women in Jeremiah 9 voiced the pain and laments that serve as a memory of the deceased. Women played a significant role in society as facilitators in the cathartic release of sorrow. They also provide a space in which they could join their voices together in a unified expression of sadness without shaming. To this end, I challenge clergies and pastors to provide space in the church for the expression of grief.

2. Cultivate spiritual practices.

Nurturing your spirit and soul through spiritual practices such as prayer, meditation, or reading scriptures and other related books can be a powerful way to reconnect with the divine and find inner peace. Gardening, nature walks, and having a pet can also be a peaceful way of interacting with God's creation.

3. Stop the inner negative thoughts.

Learn to address the inner voice of negative thoughts that lead to endless chatter. Give yourself permission to choose new positive thoughts by way of a gratitude list. Having a gratitude list of what God allowed is a great place to start. My emotional healing was accelerated when I began to thank God for 25 wonderful years with my son. The reality is that many mothers didn't have 20, 15, 10, 5 or even I year with their child before burying them. Don't let negative thoughts turn your meditation into torment.

4. Seek emotional healing.

Emotional wounds can leave deep scars on the soul, and seeking emotional healing can be an important step in achieving personal growth and self-actualization. Seek support from a therapist, counselor, or trusted friend, and work through past traumas or painful experiences. Focusing on helping others going through similar emotional wounds is highly recommended provided you have accepted your loss.

5. Practice Self-care

Taking care of your physical body through healthy eating, exercise, and rest is important in achieving wholeness. Regular exercise was a dimension of saving grace that held my body together through the six-year journey to school. Routine massages are invaluable for self-care!

6. Practice forgiveness

Letting go of unforgiveness and bitterness towards yourself or others can be a freeing and healing experience. "Anger will never disappear so long as thoughts of resentment are cherished in your soul---" John Dryden.

Conclusion

The journey to wholeness is not painless but get there anyway because of the benefit God has prepared for you aforetime. At the place of wholeness, we are no longer driven by our own selfish desires or the pressures of the world around us. We are empowered and motivated by a deep desire to honor God and follow His will. We experience extraordinary inner peace, unspeakable Joy, and contentment while sitting and learning at Jesus' feet. A place where freedom reigns, all worries and troubles vanish, hearts are mended, and poverty does not exist. Like a mother who forgets the pain of childbirth, you remembered your misery no more in Jesus' name. Psalm 16:11 exemplifies life at wholeness: "You will show me the path of life; In Your presence is the fullness of Joy; at your right hand are pleasures forevermore." At wholeness you find your voice and purpose while living in abundance thus the journey is worth your trouble!

Dr. Mary Edosomwan Biography

Dr. Mary Edosomwan received both the Doctor of Ministry and Master of Divinity degrees from Samuel DeWitt Proctor School of Theology at Virginia Union University. She also received a Post-Baccalaureate Accounting degree, a Master of Health, and Finance, Bachelor of Science in Medical Technology UT at Austin.

- Email: info@cgw.org
- Web: www.centerforgriefandwholeness.com/

Chapter 2:
Surrender: Broken for Sweetness & Purpose
By Valerie O' Gorman

The search for life's meaning continues to be a profound human experience. My journey began as a teenager. I was born and raised in Dublin, Ireland. My father was a successful businessman, and we enjoyed a very comfortable life. Growing up we attended church, but the most important things in my family were money and success. People say "money can't buy happiness;" but that's usually because they don't have much and at a young age I found that to be true, money certainly doesn't bring the happiness it promises!

The first time I heard the gospel I was twelve years old. I was on holiday at our summer house in a little fishing village, south of Dublin. A little gospel bus came into town and there was preaching and singing hymnal right there in the village square. My friends stood around laughing. But I wasn't laughing! In fact God sowed seeds that day that would not bear fruit for many years. I met my husband when we were just sweet sixteen and still at school. Even then, we were looking for answers. What is life all about? Dave was raised in a Catholic home, and I was raised in a Protestant home. Back then, that was a big deal. Both of us were disillusioned with religion and hungry for truth. We began talking to all the cults available in the streets of Dublin, but we could not find answers to our questions.

In 1980 we were married and started a family. We started a business. Life was busy. I became burdened for my children. It seemed to me like history was repeating itself! We were going after all the things that people go after money, possessions, etc. Often I would say, "But there has to be more to life than this?" Like all parents, we wanted to give our children the very best. I wanted to teach the children about God, but how could I? I didn't know God myself! I started searching. I came to a life "crisis" – I just had to have answers! One day my husband came home and found me in tears with the yellow pages out, making a list of all the churches in the area that were neither Catholic nor Protestant. I started attending a Bible church not far from our home. One night after a young preacher from Belfast preached a gospel message, I went home under a tremendous burden of sin. I knew for the first time that I needed a Saviour.

In my mind I could picture the Cross of Jesus Christ – the sacrifice that was made for me at Calvary. The Holy Spirit was at work in my heart. I was broken! All those years of searching for meaningful faith. All those questions were answered at the Cross. That night I knelt down in my home, I asked Jesus Christ to come into my life to be my Saviour. The Bible says, "I am the way, the truth and the life, no man cometh to the Father but by me." For the first time I understood why Jesus died on the cross! My life changed completely. Nothing was the same. I had a brand-new perspective. I was overwhelmed with joy and gratitude. Why had no one ever told me how I could have peace with God? I was so excited. I've never gotten over getting saved. I still feel like the luckiest person alive. "For I know the thoughts that I think toward you, saith the LORD, thoughts of peace, and not of evil, to give you an expected end." Jeremiah 29:11 (KJV)

God was after a full surrender. There were 5 crucial things He had to teach me:

1. Yielding or Surrender - John 15:16 "Ye have not chosen me, but I have chosen you, and ordained you, that ye should go and bring forth fruit, and that your fruit should remain: that whatsoever ye shall ask of the Father in my name, he may give it you." My husband and I travelled from Wisconsin to Denver to be appointed by a mission board in preparation for our return to Ireland. I had a conflicted heart. Up until this point my attitude was, "This far – No further." But God was after a full surrender! I argued with God. Afterall, I was not raised a Christian. I've no point of reference, no role model for this faith journey. Sometimes I would rely on the faith of people of the Bible. I would read Hebrews chapter 11 – the roll call of the faith, especially Abraham. What about my regrets? Joel 2:25 "And I will restore to you the years that the locust hath eaten, the cankerworm, and the caterpillar, and the palmerworm, my great army which I sent among you." What about my feelings of inadequacy? 2 Corinthians 12:9 "And he said unto me, My grace is sufficient for thee: for my strength is made perfect in weakness. Most gladly therefore will I rather glory in my infirmities, that the power of Christ may rest upon me." There was nothing for it but to return to the Cross and yield my heart afresh to God. I discovered that Yielding = happiness. The sweetness of serving God in simplicity and honesty. The great joy of being used by God.

2. Patience - James 1:3 "Knowing this, that the trying of your faith worketh patience." Sometimes the hardest person to be patient with is yourself. Especially when God is doing a deep work of healing and restoration. Again, my part is surrender. Yield to the Master's hand. Philippians 1:6 "Being confident of this very thing, that he which hath begun a good work in you will perform it until the day of Jesus Christ:"

3. Fear - Romans 8:15 "For ye have not received the spirit of bondage again to fear; but ye have received the Spirit of adoption, whereby we cry, Abba, Father." The opposite of faith

is fear. God used my love for my children and wanting their best to draw me to himself. The enemy used fear to try to stop me. Fear of the future. Fear for their security. Again I had to surrender and choose to believe God. The enemy wants you in bondage – God wants you free.

4. A Clean Heart - 1 John 1:9 "If we confess our sins, he is faithful and just to forgive us our sins, and to cleanse us from all unrighteousness." I discovered I needed a clean heart for full usefulness. We cannot hide from God ~ we cannot hide our sin. I. Do you need cleansing? II. Do you have the joy of the Lord or is something sapping your spiritual energy? III. Is there some sin you are covering up? IV. What sin burden do you tolerate? Why? V. Has the enemy got you where he wants you? VI. God wants us to know sweet fellowship with Him – the abundance, the transparency of a clean heart given to God. VII. God promises to forgive us fully – if we confess our sins to Him. VIII. Christ died to deliver us from sin. IX. Repent – Forsake – Move on! I want a life God can bless! I want God's power! I want a life above the ordinary. My first step – Surrender.

5. Pilgrim Mentality - Hebrews 11:8-10 "By faith Abraham, when he was called to go out into a place which he should after receive for an inheritance, obeyed; and he went out, not knowing whither he went. By faith he sojourned in the land of promise, as in a strange country, dwelling in tabernacles with Isaac and Jacob, the heirs with him of the same promise: For he looked for a city which hath foundations, whose builder and maker is God." I heard a speaker once ask, "What are you going to do with your one little life?" It got me thinking. We are only pilgrims. We are just passing through. Our final destination is the City of God.

Six weeks later, my husband didn't want to know! "It's fine for you, but it's not for me," he said. Like a lot of Irish people he had had enough of religion. I left Bible tracts all over the house, or my Bible opened to gospel passages on the coffee table in the living room. When the pastor came to visit, my husband would disappear out to the yard and busy himself with something or other. His attitude was – I don't need this! I'm a good person! In desperation, the pastor left a Q&A sheet on the 10 Commandments. When he came to the question, "Have you ever told a lie?" The Holy Spirit shone a light on all the sin in my husband's life. He realized he was a sinner in need of a Saviour. That night he asked Jesus to save him. The following day he called and asked me to meet him in McDonalds. He asked me not to embarrass him! I dared not hope! I wondered what this meant? When I arrived he said – last night I trusted Christ as my Saviour. I was ecstatic! I jumped up and hugged him. Of course, I embarrassed him – I cried with gratitude. Now we were united in Christ. The future looked very bright.

Six weeks later, Dave woke me in the middle of the night. He's not one for the drama – this was very unlike him. He told me that God was calling him to preach. In confusion, I said, "Go back and ask Him again! Maybe you heard him wrong." He explained that his heard was heavy for all those around us who needed the Gospel. What did this mean? What was God asking of us? We had never known anyone who was called to preach. We went through a time of questioning and doubt. We knew this would mean leaving Ireland for training in Bible college in America. I wistfully stood at the kitchen window, looking at the tire swing hanging from the tree. All my girlish dreams of home, family and security seemed in jeopardy. What about my kids? What about my widowed mother? Our decision would impact so many people. We were in conflict as to our future. We cried out to God.

Dave went into the mountains to fast and pray. He returned triumphant! We will go to America – We will follow Him no matter what! He pulled a feather from his pocket. This will remind us of the decision we made today. And so we began to make our plans. In eighteen months, we had sold our home, our business, and everything we owned and went off to Bible College in Wisconsin. Our baby was only three months old when we went away. God had a lot to teach us! He was after a deeper surrender. Our families were not happy about us leaving. It was a very difficult time. Shortly after I arrived in Wisconsin, as predicted by my doctor in Dublin, I began to struggle with the transition to living in the U.S. Postnatal depression was the diagnosis. As the darkness descended; I became more and more isolated. It was the dark night of the soul. There are so many misconceptions about depression. People often think it's about tears, sadness even despair, and so often it is. But I did not know that often as depression deepens, there is distortion and disorientation. This was very frightening to me. I was losing my hold on everything that made my life meaningful. I couldn't make sense of our decision to come to the U.S.! I couldn't make sense of being a mother with three children in very reduced circumstances, I felt completely overwhelmed.

One night I went out in the car. I just drove out of town and kept driving. I was at my very lowest. I felt I just couldn't go on. That night I thought about ending it all. I thought about driving my car off a bridge. I thought about my baby back at the apartment. I thought about my other two kids. I thought about my husband and the vision he had to return to Ireland as missionaries to preach the gospel. I pulled the car over in a flood of tears. I was out in the middle of nowhere! Where do I go from here? I cried out to God – God spoke to me right there, "Allow me to be God in your life. Trust me. Allow me to dwarf your circumstances." When God becomes big – the circumstances become small. I surrendered that night. I returned home to my family that night a different person. I had met with God. I had made a full surrender. We were in the U.S.

for almost 5 years. The last eighteen months we were on deputation preparing to return to Ireland.

This was a challenging time; Dave was still in college, and I was home schooling 3 young children. We returned to Ireland in 1992. Dave was called to pastor the church we had been saved into. We have now been serving at Lifegate for 32 years. It is a great privilege to serve the Lord. He is worthy. We thank God for his faithfulness to us. When God breaks us, it is always with a purpose in mind. To be broken of self-dependence and self-reliance is a painful process. Our pride is a huge barrier to a surrendered God-centered life. If I was going to fashion a tool fir for the Master's use I would first need to remove anything that would hinder full usefulness. I would remove the deadwood, to release the new life. I was crushed to release a sweet fragrance of Jesus.

Many years ago someone gave me a copy of the book *The Prayer of Jabez*. I began to pray the little prayer, "Multiply for thy glory the influence of my household" over my family. I didn't really understand what that prayer meant. Now over 20 years later, I see God's hand in the lives of my children. All of my children are serving the Lord. My grandchildren are beginning to step up, wanting to follow Jesus. Recently at a family gathering I looked over the heads of my children bowed in prayer, and I remembered the tire swing in the backyard all those years ago. Sacrifice means – giving to another what you would like to keep for yourself. My decision to trust Christ changed the direction of our whole family in this generation, and for generations to come. "Looking unto Jesus the author and finisher of our faith; who for the joy that was set before him endured the cross, despising the shame, and is set down at the right hand of the throne of God." Hebrews 12:2 KJV

Valerie O'Gorman Biography

Valerie O'Gorman is a coach and international guest speaker! She has been a pastor's wife for more than 30 years in Dublin, Ireland; where she has developed a thriving women's ministry. She also has a background in early childhood education and special needs education. Valerie's passion is breaking the chains that bind and leading people to a life of victory in Christ.

- Email: ogormanvalerie@gmail.com
- Facebook: Valerie O'Gorman
- LinkedIn: linkedin.com/in/valerie-o-gorman-a1920617b

Chapter 3:
Follow the Money, Diary of a Patient, Her Doctors, and Big Pharma
By Ann LeMaster

My story comes to you from my health background and education. I describe myself as a "late bloomer". I enlisted in the US Military at the age of 31, became a nurse at 45, and at 72 years old, I launched my current career as an Inspirational Speaker, Podcast Host and Author. I grew up in Iowa, USA, in the 1950's. I was raised with values, respect and "critical thinking" skills. I am so thankful for my strict upbringing. I have a voracious appetite to learn and a passion for sharing my knowledge with anyone who wants to listen. I learned much about nature and our human connection to All that Is. We ate off the land from what we raised. My mother's family knew Homeopathy and the healing abilities of foods and herbs. As a family unit we worked together, each having our "chores".

As a sickly child, any disease that went around, I got, as with the flu pandemic in 1957. Two weeks later I got the flu again. I haven't had the Flu since the pandemic of 1968! At eight years old I was very sick and was bed-ridden for two and one-half months. That is when I decided I wanted to be a nurse. I liked the nurse that was so nice and took care of me and I wanted to be just like her, helping people. Thirty-six years later, I received my diploma. My medical knowledge and my common sense have ruled my life for over fifty years! I eat healthy (80 % organic, 20% human). I refuse to get sick! My attitude is, "What you think about you bring about." I instruct my body to think positive thoughts and I refuse to live in fear! I do not allow FEAR in my life. Fear is a negative vibration (emotion) that lowers your immunity and invites disease. I do not allow fear in my life. Do you?

I listen to my body speak to me. Intuitively, (God's gift), I know what it needs or wants. My body has served me well over the years and I certainly have abused it, whether through carrying 60- pound circuit breakers, emptying a pick-up load of dirt in a day, hauling the dirt to my garden, or dancing four hours on Friday nights for enjoyment and socialization. I didn't always use proper body mechanics when working. Instead, I have always had a mindset of "got to get 'er done". Wear and tear of using my body for manual labor has taken its toll.

Two years ago, at 71 years old, I was in a deep squat position for too long, planting my garden plants before the storm hit. I must have pulled some muscles because I was in agony! Modern medicine has a pain scale of one to ten, with ten being the most painful. I have a very high pain tolerance of thirteen. I endured the pain for three months until my next doctor's appointment. I told her my issue and her response was offering Prednisone, NSAIDs or therapy. I said therapy, and asked why was that the last modality offered? It should have been the first! I went to therapy and didn't get relief until I pinpointed an area on the back of right my hip. The therapist identified it as "IT Band". At last, I said, we can get something done about it! I was to do exercises.

I previously had a left hip replacement from an injury twenty-two years earlier. Every year I see the hip surgeon. When he said "surgery" after I told him my leg issue, I responded with "for an I T Band?" I suggested an X-ray since I was there, but he said, "We'll wait till next year." 'Why wait?' I thought. I am done with him.

Follow the money!

I continued with the therapy. I didn't get any better. In fact, I got much worse. The pain now radiated down my leg to my knee. I was still getting worse, as the tenderness and pain traveled from my pelvis, thigh, to my knee and settled into my ankle as well. I was now walking with a limp! By now I lost muscle mass and was beginning to feel my age. I was feeling like a crippled old woman!

Intuitive guidance, once again, came to my rescue, as cannabis (marijuana). Cannabis has been outlawed in the U.S. for decades. It has recently come upon the scene as being therapeutic. A seed-based nutritional company I am involved with has developed a CBD balm. I rolled it on my leg and crossed my fingers, hoping for relief. Fifteen minutes later, the relief came. Wonderful! No pain, although it didn't last, just temporary relief. But I knew I was on the correct path.

Alternative medicine

Still in tune to my body's guidance, I knew I needed a deep tissue massage. Unfortunately, insurance does not pay for alternative modalities, apparently only for Pharmaceuticals. That is where the REAL money is! Do you get the picture "they" don't want us fixed? It was breaking my "rainy-day-fund" going every week, for a beneficial modality in the form of massage. Several months later, the therapist went elsewhere. Now, I had to find someone else to help me.

I found a female therapist who happened to be Trigger Point Therapist. I had a very painful spot on the web of my right hand (between the thumb and first finger) which needed trigger point therapy to release the pain. Because I give shots and perform Bio-Metric Screenings, as well as my garden "play time", I need my fingers to perform both functions. The pain was so intense that I was concerned. I was wondering how much longer I would be able to do my job? One trigger point treatment from the therapist and it hasn't bothered me since!

I didn't go to her for that, so it was a plus that she fixed it. I wonder what drug the doctor would have offered for that pain? The Therapist suggested to me my issue was Sciatica and recommended a colleague, Jay.

At this current writing I've been seeing Jay now, every ten days or so for about three months. He explained where I was in my process of healing and where he could get me to. He explained that Sciatica leads to Scoliosis, a back deformity. That made sense to me. It's as though the muscle gets so tight for too long and pulls the spine out of position. We need to exercise our whole body to keep our muscles optimal!

My Epiphany

My "rainy-day fund is now depleted but I am grateful. I am able to MOVE my body into positions I haven't been able to for two years! I'm once again able to exercise and I have begun to regain the muscle mass I lost these past months. I have my sanity back! I feel 50 again! If my muscles were stronger, I could dance all night! I am not completely healed, but I am well on my way. Hope is ALIVE! I have a doctor's appointment this week with a new doctor, an Osteopath. I pray this doctor cares about the health of his patients, not about the kick-back they pocket from drug prescriptions.

I just returned from my new doctor's appointment. An MRI is scheduled in 2 weeks. Currently, his diagnosis is Osteoarthritis, from wear and tear. No matter the outcome, I will survive it with a winning attitude.

Upon Reflection

Now, why didn't the hip replacement doctor order this six months ago? More money in a surgery is my guess. Scenario: (1) Prescription is written, (2) patient fills said prescription at pharmacy, (3) Pharmaceutical company makes more pills and other medications, and the cycle continues. The doctor, the pharmacy, and the pharmaceutical company all "got paid" and the patient, due to side-effects of the first pill, is now on 3-10 medications, and feels un-well. I refuse to "play that game"!

In fairness to doctors; I knew a drug representative (now deceased). We talked about how he was instructed to market drugs to doctors. If a doctor asked a question pertaining to safety issues or side effects, he was to "skirt around" the issue (like a politician does). His sales volume diminished because he developed a conscience, meaning that he could not justify telling half-truths. He retired and was a much happier man.

My grandmother died from complications of Diabetes, and I swore I would not get it! Last year, I spent a month visiting family up north. They eat NOTHING healthy and have various health issues. I threw caution to the wind and forced myself to eat what they did. The following month my A1C was 5.9! The very next day I changed my diet back to what I usually eat. Six weeks later, my A1C was 4.9! The power of real foods! You have the POWER to change your life to be the best it can be. You CAN be free of medication! Make wise choices!

Medical Facts Revealed

I'm intrigued by real science, not the manipulated "fake" science recently being promoted. Modern medicine is wonderful when used for healing, not based on the pocketbook, commonly referred to as money. Do you think I sound cynical? But my views come from common sense and experience, whether my own or knowledge of another's dilemma.

In the mid-1980's, my nursing class was asked the following question, "Which function for our bodies is more important, the brain or the gut?" Of course, it's the brain, right? Afterall, that's what we've been taught all these years. Turns out, it's the gut. Fast forward to today. How many years have we been consuming chemically laden foods? By that, I mean red dye, fake sugar, etc., all destroying our gut. Speaking of fake sugar, you know which I'm talking about, the packets at every restaurant. Are you aware that synthetic sugars contribute to weight gain and ill health?

Why does a no/low-calorie sweetener cause weight/fat gain? My inner knowing "told" me several years ago. The liver's job is to detoxify our bodies. Drinking or eating toxic foods and beverages overwhelms the liver! You eat the chemical laden food, and the liver has to clean up after your body assault. We get into trouble because we don't eat just one toxic food, we eat and drink it all day long! The liver just can't keep up! It eliminates one toxin, and you ingest many more than one. Now you are fat and feel depressed. Not to worry, there is a pill for that too! Get the picture? Take charge of your life. I see our world-wide system as corrupt. Big Business creates the junk food (for profit) which makes us unwell. We go to the doctor who prescribes a pill or procedure to "fix" us. Handsome profit made from your misery; don't you agree?

In the 1980's, I was at the drag races on a hot summer day. Standing by the car, eyes on the track, I picked up a bottle of diet soda and took a swig. I gagged on it! It was warm and tasted like some chemical I've never ingested! I couldn't spit it out fast enough! I never drank another one. That experience is one of the ways I have educated myself to decipher truth. Did you know that soda should NEVER be in the sun? I've seen cases of soda at gas stations in full sun. The heat breaks the soda down into toxins. Aspartame had been pulled from a popular soda company due to health warnings. It was put back into the sodas "because the public demanded it." That was a direct quote from HR of said soda company. The real reason was most likely sales (profit) plummeted, due to taste.

Money has become the driver of our world. Sadly enough, even in the workplace profits are put before people. The job gave me enough aches and pains, and the company doctor put me on pharmaceutical medications to cover up the dis-ease I was feeling, so I would be able to continue to produce on the job. Nothing to make me well, do just enough to get me back to being profitable for the company. In fact, the last drug that the company doctor had me on--I believe it was Vioxx— was pulled from the market. It was so unsafe! Five deaths were reported. I had told the company doctor I had double-vision while taking it. He gave me a look of disgust. Afterall, in his eyes, I felt he thought of me as "just a factory worker". I reminded him that it was the last side-effect listed under the drug in the Nurses Drug Book.

Have you noticed that there is a PILL for nearly every ailment diagnosed? If you choose not to take a pill, there is bariatric surgery. Having bariatric surgery, though, doesn't give you free rein to eat whatever you want. You really can't eat much as part of your stomach has been removed. Now that you can't eat a lot, you don't consume enough to nourish your body and you will develop nutrient deficiencies as a result. There is another pill(s) for that too. And the cycle continues. I learned that I have to listen to what my body says and that there is help available. Don't just go by what the doctor tells you. Be responsible. Be your own advocate for your health. Do your research, seek out alternative options and modalities. Don't allow someone else to manage your body. Own your body!

As a result of my painful experiences with the doctors and big pharma, I have created a 3-month course that is designed to help those who are suffering with diabetes, are diagnosed as prediabetic or want to avoid the disease altogether so that they would have a better quality of life.

Ann LeMaster is a Nurse, Certified Health Coach, inspirational speaker, author, podcast host. As a nurse and Certified Health

Ann LeMaster Biography

Coach, Ann LeMaster really cares about her welfare. About YOUR welfare as well and so she wrote this story about how she was treated in our modern-day medical system. Ann has always listened to her body "speak" to her. Common sense and critical thinking skills allowed her to seek answers that the doctor may not offer. Our food is tainted and much of it is fake, as in artificial dyes and sugar-free sweeteners, which are toxic and lead to obesity, diabetes, and ill health. What you just read is a sample of the information contained in this chapter. We must be responsible for our own health. Sometimes we must see several different health care providers before we find the right one. Taming Diabetes differently is the course Ann has developed to assist you to your optimal health.

BONUS
In appreciation for your purchase of this book, I am including your choice of either:
One session on my Common Sense Living Podcast, or:
20% off the 3-month Taming Diabetes…..differently course

- Email: tamingdiabetes@yahoo.com
- Facebook: www.facebook.com/ann.master.39
- Instagram: @annthemasterhealer

Chapter 4:
The Power of Forgiveness
By Dr. Carmia Hines

It was about four years earlier when we met. I walked into the club with my girlfriend, and, within minutes, he approached me. I could tell that he had swag. He was from the local area, and I was not. For the next couple of hours, we talked and danced. He later asked, "Why is someone that looks like you still single?" My response was I am single because I have not found anyone worthy of me. He responded, "Oh well let me see what I can do about that." The night ended with him walking me to my car under his umbrella. Approximately two weeks later, I met his family over Christmas dinner. He wanted a relationship. The attraction was undeniable. Aside from his good looks, I was attracted by the fact that he took me to church with him. I did not need to ask. He led. I had assured myself and my mother that I was done with marriage. Yet, within 16 months, I was engaged and remarried.

As divorcees, with almost 35 years of marriage between us both, we agreed there was no need for premarital counseling. I would later begin questioning that decision. One weekend while watching a movie my handsome, smart, Christian husband made an insulting comment to which I retorted, "What's good for the goose is good for the gander." He insultingly came back with, "Sounds like you have a get back spirit." I could have taken offense, but just laughed it off and opted to give him grace, knowing that according to Romans 3:23. NKJV... "all have sinned and fall short of the Glory of God." What had I learned, if anything, from my previous marriages? Without some instruction on what might have gone wrong before, why would I think I could get marriage right this go around? I was the same woman just marrying a different, better man.

Although, I understood the importance of living and learning from mistakes. Still, I didn't seek help. And without help or teaching, I forged forward. I had it all in the bag. Or so I thought.

Games People Play

My husband and I often talked about various topics. We shared about past pains. Since childhood, I had become intolerable of aggression, lying, or cheating in any of my relationships, such that, I developed a suspicious mindset. So, I found myself periodically asking questions like, "Who was that texting you last night?" or "Where else did you go?" Despite my gut feelings that something was amiss, I wanted to believe everything in our marriage was good. Ultimately, I accepted his explanations. I am thinking, I'm sharing my life with this wonderful man. We are both Christians with mutual appreciation for each other. Yet, I continued to be plagued by the thought that something was wrong. We rarely associated with other married Christians. I began to recognize, from questionable behaviors on his part, that our mindsets differed when it came to interacting with the opposite sex. I understood the importance of having reliable relationships in my life. I believe what was missing in this marriage was associating with like-minded Christians of shared values. I wanted a married Christian woman to share my feelings with.

Boundaries

Hoping I had not made another mistake, I was trying to manage my emotions. My thoughts kept running wild. By this point, our married lifestyle was primarily church attendance, occasional alcohol drinking and spending time with old friends. This day, he was headed back home from a weekend basketball tournament with old friends. My telephone rang. To my surprise, it was a female voice telling me that my husband does not care about me. My heart sank. This anonymous voice continued, "He does not love you." Hours later, my husband arrived back home. Meeting him at the door, I asked about his trip and shared the phone call I had just received. I could not ignore his nonverbals or fidgeting. I became furious, exploded, then threw and shattered a valuable vase. I had been here before, knowing the difference between reacting and responding. Although my flesh wanted to lash out, I chose the latter and we talked. My husband denied any cheating and agreed to discontinue annual tournament trips. Within months life went on, as usual. Months later, another inappropriate incident happened. I said NOT AGAIN!!

My Choices! My Baggage! Our Deliverance!

Galatians 5:19 NKJV — Now the works of the flesh are evident, which are: adultery, fornication, uncleanness, lewdness…. Then, out of nowhere, it happened! We were attending a formal social for my husband's job, when a woman approached us standing in a group. She immediately began rubbing my husband's bald head and smiling. In total disbelief at his inaction, I froze with my eyes fixed upon his face. I would have expected him to at least question her actions and step backward from this woman's hand. I was enraged. In my mind, I saw my fist striking my husband's face. I was saying in my mind, 'I cannot take this.' Instead of leaving the party abruptly, I chose to wait. I was at my wits end. I asked him, who and what was that? My husband insisted there was nothing between him and the female coworker. I gave my husband a few choice words ending with, "You need help." We rode home virtually in silence.

At home, I said "Get out. I am going to file for a divorce!" What happened next surprised me. My husband responded, "I love you. I do not want a divorce. I am not leaving." The words cut me, and I was furious. My husband had often referred to me as being more spiritually mature than himself, but in tears, I repeated, "You need to get some help." He responded, "I will find help, sleep on the couch, whatever, but not leave." He continued with, "I love you and will do what I need to keep you." I did not expect his response and grew more frustrated. I was uninterested in his words; they merely elevated my fury thinking my husband is a liar and a cheat. I felt I had seen it all before, as a young girl. Now, I had been betrayed. I was thinking, 'I will not stay in this mess.' I had been divorced and seen the chaos it could produce. I stood firm on my "deal breakers". Divorce is "the only option". I had not anticipated him volunteering to sleep on the couch. I was surprised by his willingness to do whatever it took to make things right (again) between us.

The more he yielded, the angrier I got. Why? Simultaneously, I felt something happening inside me. Later, I would identify The Holy Spirit watching and waiting for me to ask for help. Jesus just wanted me to be honest and say what I was thinking, 'I can't take this. I need help.' What was wrong with me? I was frustrated at his saying that he wanted to work on our marriage. 2 Corinthians 10:3-4 NKJV — For though we walk in the flesh, we do not war according to the flesh. For the weapons of our warfare are not carnal but mighty in God for pulling down strongholds. The next day, my husband immediately contacted our church for counseling. He called each day until he received a return call where he was instructed to be at next week's Men's Bible study. Over the next several weeks, he attended Bible study, slept on the couch, and heard my short fuse. At the same time, I cried, prayed, studied God's Word, and sought out Bible messages to speak to my situation. The more time I spent with God, the more tears I shed. Jesus was touching my heart.

My understanding of what God needed from me was conflicting with what I wanted. God wanted me to give more grace to my husband and I wanted him to feel my pain. One night at dinner, not recalling what he said to me, I annoyingly replied, "I have been thinking of contacting my ex and have no doubt he will take me up on it." My husband irritatingly replied and abruptly ended dinner. I continued reading the Bible and in worship, the Holy Spirit began showing me myself. He was prompting me that He wanted to use me to help my husband with his struggles. I was feeling an intolerable pain and wanted the ordeal to end. I confessed Jesus, as a child, was baptized in the Holy Spirit and knew what was right in God's eyes. Still, I had spent years going at life my own way. I had neglected my relationship with Jesus and lived disobediently.

Later, we went to see the church counselor together. He told her what I had said and her response to me was, "You don't want that." The counselor went on suggesting that I read a particular book about betrayal, hope, and healing. Spending time studying, praying, worshiping, and releasing my truth to God helped me begin seeing clearer. I had been aching trying to use what I could, including men, to cope. Now, I was seeing some places in my life only God had the power to satisfy. I had been desiring what only God was going to be able to fulfill. My Bible and that book became my best friends.

Psalm 37:4 NKJV — Delight yourself also in the LORD, And He shall give you the desires of your heart. I began to hunger for understanding of what it was that I really had been craving. How did my own desires line up with God's plans for me? God was revealing that my soul was out of alignment with His plan. He created me. He knew me best. I was unwilling. Romans 8:28 NKJV — And we know that all things work together for good to those who love God, to those who are the called according to His purpose. In the months following, I continued reading, hearing and now actually listening. I fell to the floor and wept. I can only contrast giving birth to my daughter. Although I did not have an epidural, my memories of becoming a mother are filled with happiness. Conversely, in this case, my flesh was working hard against God's desire to use me. God wanted to produce new fruit in and through me, in my husband, in our marriage. My mind and body wanted to be in control, "to win my way". I had watched my mother and late father's marriage and believed my siblings did similarly. I confess to being a work in progress and saw something was not right back then. I would get angry at times, saying to myself, one day I would do marriage differently.

A Christian, teen mother, and wife, I often considered my mom's endurance in marriage. Her goals were to graduate her children from high school and that they be born from one husband. God promises to always work things out for those called His own. I am encouraged seeing that God has gone beyond what my mother asked of Him.

The Greatest of These is Love

John 15:10-11 NKJV — "If you keep My commandments, you will abide in My love, just as I have kept My Father's commandments and abide in His love. "These things I have spoken to you, that My joy may remain in you, and that your joy may be full. I willingly entered the marriage without any formal counseling or accountability. I knew God. While this chaos ensued in my marriage, many tears fell, and I prayed. I began listening to Him asking me rhetorically, "Who are you? Where is grace? I gave the gift of grace to you, and now you have none to spare for your husband. He is the man you vowed to love. I gave you as a help to him. If not you, then who? What will happen? You use your gifts, serving thousands in the military and your business. How much more of a priority is your husband/fellow brother in Christ? Do you not have enough love for him?"

I began thinking, if I cannot help my husband, then who? From where will my husband draw his hope? Hebrews 4:16 NKJV — Let us therefore come boldly to the throne of grace, that we may obtain mercy and find grace to help in time of need. God asks that we love one another, even those who use us. I am a sinner, in need of love and grace. God met and continues meeting me at my place of need. I was attempting to hold my husband to a higher standard. My husband was asking for grace, help and forgiveness. I was struggling to forgive. With God's help, I began to see my husband as Jesus saw me. He sees me as His own, accepted and beloved, as I am. Had I forgotten God's Promise of Love and Hope? Ephesians 2:8-9 NKJV — For by grace you have been saved through faith, and that not of yourselves; it is the gift of God, not of works, lest anyone should boast.

My husband, never knowing his birth mother and rejected by his paternal grandmother, had been struggling with his own deep-rooted feelings of worthlessness. How must he feel? For the first time in our marriage, I began listening intently. God wanted me to Love my husband in HIS strength. I had been trying to love my husband on my own. Philippians 2:13 NKJV — for it is God who works in you both to will and to do for His good pleasure. We had both prioritized our feelings over needs in our marriage. We sought help that disclosed personal battles. The Holy Spirit provided a fresh perspective to our marriage. God wants marriage to reflect His nature. Husbands are to love their wives and wives are to respect their husbands. We are gifts to each other in carrying out God's plan for marriage. Jeremiah 29:11 NKJV — For I know the thoughts that I think toward you, says the LORD, thoughts of peace and not of evil, to give you a future and a hope.

My husband and I continually share our story of renewal and hope. As Couples Ministry Mentors and God's Word as basis, we help married couples identify and navigate common barriers to living out marriage His way. God is using our marriage to help upbuild His Kingdom and develop disciples. As assistant Class Facilitators of Conflict Resolution and Couples Discipleship courses, we share tools to help husbands and wives stand on their vows, as God has promised to love and never leave us. Galatians 5:22-23 NKJV — But the fruit of the Spirit is love, joy, peace, longsuffering, kindness, goodness, faithfulness, gentleness, self-control. Against such there is no law.

Dr. Carmia Hines Biography

Dr. Carmia Hines is a Small Business owner, Mary Kay Independent Beauty Consultant. She is committed to providing superior service teaching women and men to consistently care for themselves. She is a University Mentor for The School of Sciences at two Colleges. Dr. Hines is a retired Air Force Officer and Disabled Veteran having served over 24 years on Active Duty. Retired Major Hines has over a dozen military medals, decorations and awards from Finance and Healthcare Career Fields. Dr. Hines holds an Associate of Science (AS) degree in Financial Management, from the Community College of the Air Force, a Bachelor of Science (BS) degree in Management Studies, from the University of Maryland University College, a Master of Science (MS) degree in Human Relations, from the University of Oklahoma. Dr. Carmia is a Doctor of Philosophy in Psychology, with an Industrial/Organizational Psychology specialization.

- Email: Hinesc68@yahoo.com
- Website: http://marykay.com/chines7761
- LinkedIn: www.linkedin.com/in/carmia-sykes-hines-06a88989

Chapter 5:
The Handing Over of a Diamond
By Cindy-Ann Lewis

January 2011, I was parking my daughter's lunch bag for school when I heard quietly but clearly, "When you are finished packing this lunch bag, I want you to go upstairs, dress in exercising clothes and walk with Diamond down the road to catch the school bus. I want you to wait with her until the bus arrives, kiss her goodbye then start walking in the direction of the Good Hope Swimming Pool, down to the main road, pass the St. Paul's Police station, down to the Greens, up Mardigras road and back to your home, but before you leave, take the book of faith with you." Now, if you knew me well, you will have known that I was not a person who was easily motivated to exercise, shamefully so. I didn't like feeling too sweaty and yes, I live in the tropics. Yet suddenly, I was overwhelmed by a feeling of excitement that sent me sprinting up the stairs to my bedroom. There, I jumped into exercising clothes and was about to fly down the stairs when I screeched to a halt.

"Wait Lord, what do you mean by take the book of faith with you?" I asked. "I am referring to Hebrews chapter 11. Read it before you leave and meditate on it as you exercise. Do this every morning as you go out with Diamond to get the school bus and continue to exercise." So, rushing to get my Bible, I rustled through the pages and finding the chapter, I quickly scanned through it before leaving for my new adventure. Exercise. Yes! God knew I needed that. As I started walking with Diamond, she looked at me quizzically and asked, "Mummy, are you going to walk with me today to get the bus?" "Yes," I replied. "Yeaaaaa," she chirped in excitement. "Mummy will you wait with me until the bus arrives?" "Yes," I replied again. "Yeaaaaa," she chirped again in sheer excitement. The bus came and so we hugged. I kissed her, waved goodbye then started on my walk, all the way, thinking about the men of faith in Hebrews 11.

It was by faith that these people believed God and it was counted as righteousness. Whoa! And Abel, even though the man had died, yet his obedience was so outstanding that it still speaks to us today! What a testimony from God! Selah. Next day I awoke with my heart filled with joy, eagerly embracing the challenge again, then the next day and the next. The days were turning into weeks, and I was feeling good about myself. Sunday, March 13th arrived. It was the day before my birthday, and it was fully adorned with excitement which exploded into fun and fits of laughter as I celebrated this birthday that year. As I reflect, listening to the sound of the children's mischievous jokes as they wrestled with each other and made their bid for the biggest piece of BBQ pork, Madam Diamond being the loudest, was nothing short of a musical masterpiece. By evening however, that music was suddenly replaced by dread trumpeting through all the happy bliss. In fact, I was just about to explore the sumptuous flavors of my meal when I was interrupted by my niece as she exclaimed, "Diamond, you're looking funny! How is it that your eyes are yellow?" "Ah looking funny?" retorted Diamond, "You en see your old, big head nuh (laughter)?"

"Diamond! For true, why is your eyes so yellow and your skin looking so black? All yuh, come and see!" "Cindy-Ann, come!" shouted my mother in panic. At the sound of her voice my heart dropped, I felt paralyzed. I looked at my sister-in-law who was sitting across the table from me, she looked at me and I immediately went into instant prayer. "Lord, whatever this is, please, strengthen me to deal with it." Diamond had complained about stomach pain and fatigue a few weeks before. I had taken her to the doctor who ran some tests, but the results came back as normal. In fact, two days before this birthday party I had taken her to another doctor because she had again complained that her stomach was not feeling well. This doctor did not think that there was anything to worry about except that her body was preparing for menstruation or maybe she had eaten something bad from school sports the day before. The fact that she was feeling well on Sunday and having so much fun was certainly comforting. Yet, little did I know that we were entering into the storm of our lives!

What was wrong? Was there something that was overlooked? After pulling myself together, I too went to see what was causing all the uproar. What I saw caused me to grab the phone and immediately call her pediatrician who eventually summoned me to take her to the emergency care of the General Hospital, stressing the fact that yellow eyes are an indication that there is an issue with the liver. As we drove somberly from our home (party crashed), Diamond, astonished and confused by the drama kept affirming that she was feeling very well. On the route, we made a detour to our church Evangelistic Crusade in Grandmal and requested prayer from the Evangelist before heading for the hospital. That night, she was admitted, leaving us confused and in shock.

The day, March 14th, broke through the dark clouds of despair from the night before, filling our hearts with anxious hope as we hurried to the hospital eager to meet with the doctors and to bring comfort to our only child. "Don't worry too much mummy," I was told by one doctor. "We will run a few tests and in no time Diamond should be out of here." What comfort! After all, she was not a sickly child. However, by the next day Diamond's body had changed, her legs and tummy were showing signs of swelling and her condition had worsened by day four. There was no doubt that something was terribly wrong, and the doctors were scrambling to get answers. To further frustrate the situation, Diamond's blood had to be sent to a lab in the neighboring island Trinidad for various testing as our health care was inadequately equipped to offer the testing required at the time.

After paying her lab fees through the bank, I returned to the lab in the General Hospital to drop off the receipt. As I turned to leave, I asked, "How soon can we expect the result?" The answer that I received exploded in my head sending every thought and expectation flying into hopelessness! I was told that I should have the results in four to six weeks! What? Who had time to wait for this eternity? I did not want to imagine what could happen while she waited. Bolting out of that place, I sped home and flung myself on the couch. There I lay trying to calm my nerves; struggling not to drown in anger and disappointment. Then, out of seemingly nowhere, I heard in a quiet but calm voice, "Why are you so chastised over Diamond's situation?" "Why should I not be?" I retorted. "Can't you not see what is happening to her Lord?" I asked. "Yes, came the answer, but why are you chastised?" "Lord, Lord..." I stuttered through tears. He continued, "Why are you allowing the enemy to chastise you for your peace when I was already chastised for it? I took the chastisement of your peace upon me at Calvary so that you can enjoy peace now and even in the worst of situations."

Convinced that the Holy Spirit was ministering to me, I sat up, wanting to hear more. I eventually made a dash for my Bible, dropped on the floor, my mind flooding with the light of His Word as He continued to speak. "So many Christians are quoting my word: But He was wounded for our transgression, He was bruised for our iniquities: The chastisement of our peace was upon Him: and by his stripes we are healed (Isaiah 53:5). Yet too many believers do not understand what it means. In fact, when loved ones die, believers mourn just like the world, as if there is no hope. There is hope, believers can have peace if only they will trust Me." Then in a sad voice I heard, "I am looking for someone who will show off my peace." Selah. He sounded sad. I felt grieved that He was sad, so wanting to please Him I shouted, "Me Lord! Me! I will show off that peace for You! Give me that peace and I will show it off for You." Before you knew it, I was on a 'spiritual high' rebuking the devil and marching around my living room praying and laying bold claim to that peace. It was mine, Jesus suffered so that I can have it, so I wanted it. I declared this over and over, filling my heart with faith whilst recalling Hebrews chapter 11 and the men who believed God.

Dear readers, please allow me to inform you that up to that point, it never crossed my mind that Diamond's illness would lead to death. I was claiming God's peace because I just wanted to live in it. Anyway, taking into consideration the doctors at the General Hospital in Grenada couldn't do much to help her through no fault of theirs, on Monday the 21st, we arrived in the island of Barbados. After seeing a Gastroenterologist, she was rushed to the hospital where she remained for three weeks. I will forever be grateful for the doctors, nurses, medical technicians who worked around the clock, desperately probing for answers that just couldn't be found and to the Humphrey family of St. Michael and my sister-in-law, Eunice who labored in providing loving support to us. It was indeed a frustrating battle, fully equipped with the incessant prayers and support of the saints, yet her life was rapidly deteriorating in front of us.

The pain was brutal and the only true comfort I could find was in God. It was my pregnancy with this child that had convinced me beyond doubt that God was real. Pregnancy revealed Him as the Creator of life, the world and everything in it. Every kick and fluttering in the womb brought a kind of fear and understanding that I needed to surrender my life to Him as well as to train up my child in the way of the Lord, which I did. Hence I was determined to ensure that I stayed as calm as I could and do all that I can to strengthen my child who had accepted Jesus as Lord and Savior the year before and had already taken some classes in preparation for water baptism. On April 7th, at 8:30 am, after an emotionally turbulent journey across the black eerie sky, we arrived in Connecticut via an air ambulance bound for a children's hospital. At 4:30 pm, Diamond succumbed to her death. Minutes before she died, I was sitting in a room with some hospital staff when suddenly I heard what sounded like the rustling sound of dry leaves blowing overhead. As I looked up to see what this was, I was powerfully uprooted from my seat and charging down the hall into Diamond's room. There was no doubt in my mind that I would lay hands on that child, and she would recover!

I had the faith but that was clearly not the will of God. For reasons beyond my power and control, I heard myself praying instead, "Father, I know you can heal Diamond from the crown of her head to the soles of her feet but if you choose not to, so be it. Father, today, I am turning my back, and I am handing her back to you." With that, I turned around and bolted out of the room, galloping like a horse, and screaming hallelujahs, psalms, praises, and every word of God that came to my remembrance. I could still recall doors flying open and persons chasing after me and pinning me down on a couch, but no one could subdue the power of God and the praise that was erupting through my mouth! Minutes later, I received news that she had passed. Words are inadequate to truly express the pain that I felt at the realization that she will no longer be seen on this earth. The shock! The horror! The dread! Alone in a cold room that night, with no family or friends, my body shook like a chicken whose head had been chopped off. Feeling like a root was detached from my stomach, I felt a strong and shattering, physical separation between me and my child.

Our Diamond had truly departed; gone too soon. My yearning for her touch and her laughter was enough to send me to the mental institution had it not been for the help of the sweet and comforting Holy Spirit reminding me about Jesus who voluntarily died on that cruel cross so that we who believe and put our trust in him can have eternal life. I was glad. Oh, what this cross had done for us! I believe I will see her again. I cherished the words that I had prayed earlier, "Father, I am turning my back and handing her back to you." In the days ahead, I saw the love of people and the evil thereof. I give God praise for my husband, relatives, the brethren, my Pastor Christopher Baker and his wife, and all who lovingly supported in some way. However, as the days passed, I became aware that there was a peace that rose above the pain. A comforting peace. So great was that peace that I was able to stand in the funeral over Diamond's dead body and proclaim the Word of God before hundreds of people, all for His glory. This was the peace that I had promised to show off for Jesus! It is a peace that surpasses my understanding. He gave it to me and without it, I am sure I could not have made it.

After the funeral, I was determined not to give up and so I kept my mind stayed on God by resuming my studies at the West Indies school of Theology (Grenada) and continuing with my life as normal. I had lost my only child, but I did not lose my faith. I eventually became Director of Women's Ministry at my church, the Evangelistic Centre. Today, I teach scripture classes at a private secondary school on the island, The St. George's Institute. When asked why I believe God is real, I testify about my greatest conviction which came through pregnancy. Today, I would like to encourage someone somewhere to make Jesus Christ their Lord and Savior before it is too late.

Cindy-Ann Lewis Biography

Cindy-Ann Sophie Lewis, a Grenadian by birth, is the daughter of Curlita and Leroy Donald of Calliste and the wife of Daniel Lewis for over twenty-seven years now. Despite the fact that she did not have a Christian upbringing, Cindy-Ann grew up in close proximity to the Calliste Pentecostal church and so her heart's desire from an early age was to become a Christian woman through simple observation of the Christian verses the unbeliever lifestyle around her. Fortunately, she surrendered her life to Christ at the age of thirty and is indeed grateful to God for granting her long life to embrace this opportunity. Since becoming a Christian, Cindy-Ann has always been actively involved in the work of the ministry and is presently serving as Director of the Women's Ministry of Evangelistic Centre, Market Hill, St. George's.

- Email: cindidannyella@gmail.com

Chapter 6:
The Entrapment of Fear into the Realization of Purpose
By Patricia Juba

My first remembrance of experiencing the spirit of fear is when I was six years old, sleeping in my bed when I felt a presence in the room that woke me up. I opened my eyes to see my oldest sister standing in the doorway of my room. It startled me so I jumped up to see what was wrong, however when I shook the sleep off my eyes and looked at her, all I could see was the face of a raccoon with dark circles and a sinister look in her eyes which scared me tremendously. I didn't know what to do, I jumped up and ran past her out of my bedroom door, down the hall, into my mother's bedroom and jumped into her bed; which of course startled my mother awake. I told her my sister was in my doorway, but her face looked funny like a raccoon. My mom got up to attend to my sister, returned to me and settled me in her bed.

The next day when I woke up, I was afraid to see my sister, however she was not in the house when I got up. I learned that she was in the hospital. I was told she wasn't feeling well. My thoughts were, 'She sure looked scary when she did not feel good.' The next time I saw the raccoon face in my sister, which is the best way that I could explain it at the time, this time she spoke, however it wasn't her voice that I heard. The voice was deeper and scratchy. The voice, from my remembrance, sounded like how a witch's voice is portrayed in the movies or TV. A new elevation of fear welled up in me when I saw the raccoon face and heard the witch-like voice. Instead of being vocal about what I was seeing and hearing, this made me so scared, it silenced me. I only told my mother who didn't say much about what I was saying, all I remember was my mom telling me, "You will be alright."

Being so young, I thought something was wrong with me. After all, I had three other sisters, and no one was saying that they saw the raccoon I saw or heard the witch's voice like I did. Nor why I wasn't seeing this in my other sisters, I just saw it in this sister, this was not only scary it was confusing. I do have to mention that when my sister wasn't ill, she was the nicest person to be around. She loved to cook and bake for the family. Unfortunately, this illness tormented my sister until her death in 1993. I learned several years later that my sister suffered from a mental health illness called manic depression. Although the mental health illness was explained to me by my mother, she did not explain the reason that I was seeing the distorted raccoon face and hearing the witch's voice in my sister. I continued to wonder who could explain what was going on with me.

I kept questioning myself, 'Was I becoming delusional? Did I cause these things to happen? What made her stand in front of my door?' The even bigger question I could never get an answer to was, 'How can I make my sister better?' Another childhood experience was when my second oldest sister took my niece and me to a Halloween party at a church in the neighborhood. As soon as I walked into the area where the party was being held, it appeared that I had been there before, although I knew that was never the case, that was the first time I had been there. The experience was very strange because it did feel like I had walked into this room before in a dream I had a few nights prior. I remembered the cold concrete floors, The tall white pillars, and a stage area smaller than one at a school auditorium.

In the dream I saw this very place where children were, and a man was standing and looking but not saying anything. What I saw in my dream a few nights before I walked into this church. When we entered, a man, what appeared to be six-foot tall, fair skin, with brown round glasses came out to greet us. This was the very man in my dream. Needless to say, this startled me. I thought, 'How this could be that I saw this man in my dreams before I even saw him in person or knew who he was?' I hardly wanted to interact in the activities that were there. I didn't share this with my sister that took us to the Halloween event, I just stayed really close to her and my niece until it was time to leave and go home which was not soon enough for me.

At that time, I did not explain what I was seeing, only because I didn't think anyone would believe me. Fear rose into silence within me. This became a pattern within me for the next 24 years. Had I only known then the scripture in Jeremiah 29:11(KJV) "For I know the thoughts that I think towards you, saith the Lord, thoughts of peace, and not of evil, to give you an unexpected end." I had no knowledge that what I was seeing was in the realm of the spiritual dimension, I was seeing the demonic. As the fear increased within me, so did the silence. The only person that I shared some things with was my mom. I remember telling my mom that I didn't understand why I was having these visions (I didn't know they were called visions at the time) or random dreams that didn't make sense to me. Nor why I was seeing places before physically being in the room: or seeing people before meeting them.

I tried to not pay attention to what I was seeing, mainly because I couldn't explain it without sounding like I was not in my right mind. I now know that the fear of being criticized by others felt like it would be the worst thing in the world.

However, I discovered that the fear of criticism was not the worst, experiencing low self-esteem and addiction was. I tried desperately to divorce myself from the dreams and sightings by entering relationships that I thought would change my focus. Maybe if I didn't think about what I was seeing or hearing and focused my time with others, I wouldn't have these experiences anymore. However, that was furthest from the truth. I still saw distorted faces and faces of animals on humans that scared me, dreams that warned me, but I chose to ignore them.

The end results were failed relationships and motherhood. One of those relationships unlocked and guided me into the world of addiction and homelessness. My wits end started my journey of addiction to hide the pain, fear and confusion that was in my life for so long. I simply didn't have the answers that I needed, nor did I know how to ask for the answers. The addiction started as part of my entertainment while at the same time hiding the pain of failed relationships and the fear of the unexplainable dreams and sights that I was seeing in people. At this time, I was a single parent which came with another set of fears, which was if I could be a good mother to my kids. Here is where my mother played an important role and kept my kids so that I could go through a program to help me regain my self-worth and not rely on any crutches that I chose as a coping mechanism. I successfully completed the twelve-step program, but in the back of my mind I sensed that there had to be something more than twelve steps but was not sure what "that" was.

After I successfully left the program, I was determined not to stop at the 12-step program even though I had no knowledge of what the next steps were. I secured new housing and had my children return to me. Still feeling that there is more to this life. There is more than just the 12-step program, there is more than just having a secure home for my children and myself to lay our heads, there is more to life than what I was expecting. After years of fear and confusion over the images I was seeing and voices that I was hearing, I had a conversation with my mom only to discover that she had the same experiences that I was having from childhood. She told me that no one ever explained what was going on to her, so she did not know how to explain it to me. Somehow, I felt a sense of relief to hear this from my mom after all the years that have passed not knowing that she had similar experiences as I did.

It wasn't long after the conversation that revealed my mother's experience that I entered my first Baptist church. This is where my life changed, this is where I was saved and filled with the Holy Spirit, this is where true transformation happened. I started studying the Word of God and was receiving revelation after revelation. I learned about the power of GOD, Jesus, and the Holy Spirit so much that I started sharing with my mother more and more. From all my sharing of the Word with my mother, she came into the church and was saved. My mother and I started to understand the realm of the spirit and how GOD had made us. In my mother's mid 80's she was able to share much more of her story with me which was so similar to what I had experienced. My mother was delivered and so was I from the entrapment of fear to freedom in the realm of the spirit. The saving power of the trinity of the GOD-head broke our generational curse that disabled our ability to freely speak out according to what GOD was showing, revealing, and speaking.

My mother lived until she was 93 freed from the bondages of Satan; she transitioned in 2015. I strongly believe that God used me to bring my mother to the Lord and break her silence from the fear and pain that she experienced through the course of her life. God also delivered me from the entrapment of fear that led to my silence. The manner that GOD delivered us both was truly amazing. Now when I look back over the course of my life, I can truly experience gratefulness for the process that GOD brought me through to get to where I am now! This whole process has ignited a passion in me to reach back to other women who have or are experiencing low self-esteem, fear and uncertainty in their lives that is keeping them from moving forward. Just when you tell yourself that no one will understand, God has a ram in the bush like he did for Abraham and Isaac in Genesis 22: 13-14, "And Abraham lifted his eyes, and looked, and behold behind him a ram caught in a thicket by his horns: and Abraham went and took the ram and offered him up for a burnt offering in the stead of his son;" who understands what we need.

I found my purpose in God who created me in the manner that he did from my very beginning. Now I can embrace and love who I am and do my best to encourage other women to seek God for the direction and understanding that they need to live and walk in freedom, victoriously in Him who has created us from the beginning. He makes things possible. Now I can stand on this scripture: Philippians 4:13, "I can do all things in Christ who strengthens me." God will strengthen you too! Six years ago, I founded the nonprofit organization called, A Life Worth Living, Corp. which was birthed from my passion to see other women healed and delivered from the bondages of yesteryear. The nonprofit services women and families transitioning from shelter to home, with basic needs for the families, housing advocacy, coat drives and other fundraisers to support the families.

In 2022, I became a Certified Leadership Coach, DISC Trainer/Consultant and Speaker through the John Maxwell Certified Leadership Team. I opened a consulting business, Growth Arise Consulting, LLC. I currently offer the DISC

Assessment and debriefing services to understand your communication style and how you experience better communication in every area of your life. If you have experienced or are experiencing fear in any capacity, and you don't see that there is a way out. Let me tell you that there is a way out and a way into the body of Christ! Just know that I am passionate about seeing women delivered and set free from the bondages of fear in all its variations. If you are someone who has seen or is seeing things that you cannot explain, I would be happy for you to reach out to me for a discussion and exchange experiences as a means of guidance through the scriptures that will help you understand what you are experiencing. You can contact me through the A Life Worth Living, Corp. If you would like to engage in one of my coaching sessions, you can contact me at Growth Arise Consulting, LLC, so we can make an appointment.

Patricia Juba Biography

Patricia Juba the Founder of the nonprofit A Life Worth Living, Corp. She serves women and families moving from shelter to home. Patricia is also a Certified Maxwell Leadership coach, trainer, and corporate facilitator. She is an ordained Christin Minister. Patricia desires to combine compassion with intentionality to serve those who desire to be intentional about their personal growth to get to their next season in their lives.

- Email: pjuba@alifeworthlivingcorp.org
- Website: alifeworthlivingcorp.org
- Email: growthariseconsultingllc@gmail.com
- Website: Growthariseconsultingllc.com
- Facebook: www.facebook.com/growthariseconsultingllc.com

Chapter 7:
Overcoming Pain in the Workplace: Aptitude, Attitude, Altitude
By Maria Veronica Rodrigues

My story focuses on pain in the workplace. Pain in the workplace is hardly ever talked about openly. It is hardly ever brought to the forefront. I felt the Lord wanted me to share this aspect of pain in an effort to help others who might be in similar situations, maybe stuck, unhappy on the job not knowing what to do. What was my pain in the workplace? "Management should not have selected her for the position." This was a statement that emanated from my peers saying their qualifications were superior to mine. How did I feel about hearing this? I felt ostracized and rejected since I was looking forward to relating with them as fellow co-workers.

How did I resolve this painful experience? First, by resigning after enduring for two years, the discomfort of knowing my peers did not wish for me to be part of the work team within this organization. Second, fully resolved by going back to the place of my pain and working among, and with the persons who rejected me. Eventually acceptance came. A reminder to me by management was that my soft skills were one of my strengths. My peers tried to make it difficult for me to perform my duties but the more they tried, the more I excelled in my work, and this infuriated them. They said mean things to me, and I was once shouted at by one of my peers upon approaching her with my department's request for stationery. "Maria Fraser! Move from in front of me!" (At the time I was married. Fraser was my wedded name.)

The persecution was ongoing for about two years which was the reason I resigned when there seemed to be no handshake forthcoming from my peers. The pain intensified when I recognized not only was it coming from peers who were situated on the second floor of the office but also coming from my closest peer situated on the top floor where our two desks were positioned in the same space. This meant I did not have recourse in the closest peer to me. I could not find a friend in her. Other mean things done to me were, they would check to see how I respond to assignments as if checking to see my style of writing and my competency in managing a matter from beginning to end. What approach I used that was different from theirs and gained me the nod over them. There was easy access to our work since registry filing was part of the office structure and staff had the authority to check those files to follow through on our respective assignments.

Another mean gesture was the office corridor gossip among these staff. I was not in this fraternity, but comments were thrown around as I walked past my peers. So much so, a staff member put up a quote over the photocopying room with these words: "Great minds discuss ideas; average minds discuss events; small minds discuss people," (Eleanor Roosevelt). This was the culture of the office at the time. I felt even more ostracized since the number of peers not wishing me well were more than I realized and what was hurtful was the one closest to me whom I had hoped would be different was part of my opposition. Notwithstanding this unwelcome work atmosphere created around me, I had to buckle down and get the job done.

What added to my pain was that management never addressed the matter directly. Management simply encouraged me in the position, and this helped me to be more aware that my work was appreciated and approved by management. My performance appraisal reports attested to my aptitude. One day I was sitting at the reception desk and the head of office was walking towards me and said, "Maria! You don't look happy. What's wrong?" I said, "I am writing about it." She said, "Don't write, come talk to me." Talk to her, I did. I was totally unprepared for the outcome. It seemed my sharing was confided with my closely positioned colleague which made it difficult and uncomfortable for me. As a young woman, at the time, in my 30's I did not have the skills to handle this behavior. There I was guarding my feelings and once I opened up about these feelings it caused me more pain. I really had a different expectation of my colleagues, both of whom were 12 years my senior. To say the least, I was disappointed.

Next, the head of office asked my boss to meet with me and my colleague with the aim of bringing about a resolution on the matter. My close colleague worked with the head of office, and I worked with the deputy head of office. This meeting made matters worse. My boss brought a hot bottle of wine to the meeting. I was distracted by this hot and not chilled wine. I am taking you to where I went internally. My focus was on the hot wine. Our meeting ended with no resolution with both of us returning to our desks the same way. My colleague was heard to have said we need to "bury the hatchet", an expression I was unfamiliar with at the time. When I inquired about its meaning, I understood it to mean, put an end to our indifferences and make peace. I took my story home to my husband seeking his advice, how do I regain or foster a good relationship with my close colleague? He said, "The world of work is an adult life. You have to learn how to manage these situations and it is entirely up to you. I would not tell you what to do or what not to do."

At the time, in the 1980s we did not use the words conflict resolution. Not knowing how to resolve the matter I opted to resign since the pain was not going away. What was worse, the situation was being fueled and undermined by other colleagues who thrived in festering these situations. The trust factor was lost for me. Who could I trust among my peers? I later realized it seemed I was in a competition, yet our tasks were different, each desk with its specific terms of reference. In looking back there was a fellow colleague who was neutral towards me and was heard many times over in the office saying trust was a missing ingredient among colleagues. Staff retreats were the means to correcting the trust factor and this is how acceptance of each other came about. Spending time together at weekend retreats and exposing staff to workshops among colleagues in sister offices in other countries allowed for staff to get to know each other and work at developing improved relations. This was the solution that corrected these deficiencies or major nuances in the office.

After resigning, some members of my family encouraged each other to start a family business, which we did and during this time I got pregnant and miscarried the baby, adding another pain to an already painful emotion. I recalled seeing my colleagues in the supermarket and would refuse to speak with them when they attempted to say something to me; that was how pained I was. I felt they undermined the situation when they could have done differently to help us bring about a peaceful settlement. During the time of personal pain of losing my baby I received a call from the Human Resource Manager from my office of resignation saying that the head of office was demitting office at the end of her term and leaving Guyana. She asked if I would be willing to speak with her on the phone. I said yes. She said she was sorry for the way she handled my matter and wished she had done differently, then asked if I would be willing to return to the organization, or if I wanted nothing to do with them. I said it had been two years and time heals. She said that should I consider returning, a vacancy existed for which she had recommended me to her successor.

I did return to the organization. The day I walked into the office I was greeted by the very colleague who caused my greatest pain, saying that the outgoing head of office said she must be sure to welcome me back properly. That she did. In this adversity, I experienced the power of answered prayer. Lesson learnt; don't magnify other people's behavior, rather, concentrate on developing your attitude which could ultimately win the other person over. I have the opportunity to help others through our shared life experiences as President of Valley of Decision Missions Guyana Incorporated which is an inner healing, deliverance, and prophetic ministry with a mandate to conduct annual praying and fasting retreats to bring about behavioral change.

Maria Veronica Rodrigues Biography

Maria Veronica Rodrigues was raised in three foster care homes in Georgetown, Guyana from age 6 until the time of her marriage at age 24. In her young years, for her, foster care connoted abandonment by her parents but in maturity she had a light bulb moment and was heard to have shouted out in her home, alone in the house, "Who says foster care or adoption is bad!" These words of 'foster care' took on a new meaning of positive assurance and encouragement as in the words of Jeremiah 29: 11 "For I know the plans I have for you, declares the Lord, plans to prosper you and not to harm you, plans to give you hope and a future."

- Email: mariaanthonyrodrigues@gmail.com
- Facebook: www.facebook.com/Mariarodrigues
- Instagram: www.facebook.com/Mariarodrigues

Chapter 8:
Overcoming Life's Twist and Turns
By Novellette Edwards

As I reminisce on my childhood days, I am reminded of how life lessons unfolded and helped me tackle the issues that could destroy my life. Withstanding the heat, I redirected, refocused, and overcame the unexpected turn of events that catapulted my life and impacted me in a way that has helped me overcome the dysfunctions that could have paralyzed me, enduring the heat, and coming out even more robust. As I think back, I am reminded of how disappointed I was at the people God put in my life to help me navigate life. Their lack of efforts to provide, protect, and care for me in my early years when I couldn't care for myself left me broken, questioning everything and even doubting myself. I started questioning God, heading down a dangerous path, choosing happiness in all the wrong places, and hanging with the wrong people.

Growing up, life was tough for my mother, having four children (three boys and me being the only girl), trying to raise us with only an elementary school education and no help from our fathers. My brothers tried to step in and become the men of the house by working to help. They were young and could only do odd jobs. My mother started dating, and her boyfriend visited our home quite often. He would look at me creepy in a way that made me very uncomfortable. Then, one day, he took advantage of the broken lock on the bathroom door; he came into the bathroom and tried to sexually assault me. He put one hand over my mouth, his tongue in my ears, and the other hand across my breasts. I was numb and dumbfounded, as I was caught off guard. The reality hit me that this was improper when I felt his disgusting tongue in my ear while touching my 16-year-old breasts.

My mother was asleep in the bedroom. I gathered the strength to kick him in his private area and began to fight him off as I ran out of the bathroom to tell my mom. I heard him yelling, "Your mom will not believe you." As I walked into her bedroom crying and told her, to my surprise, she became angry and approached me as if I had done something wrong. This devastated me, and I became angry, confused, and withdrawn. Why would she not protect me from my perpetrator? What did I do wrong? Where were my dad and brothers to protect me from this abuser? I was so hurt and angry I ran away from home to live with my aunt (my mother's only sister); my aunt was my saving grace. She showed me love and compassion, took me to church, and taught me to forgive. I did not know other young girls had the same experiences until I attended church and heard testimonies from many young girls; hearing their sexual abuse stories made me want to do something.

According to the National Crime Victimization Survey in an annual study conducted by the Justice Department, girls ages 12-16 are most at risk of sexual violence. And 25% of them are abused by family members. Girls are also more likely to experience penetrative abuse. After years of not knowing who my father was, he suddenly appeared. He was battling his demons, having children with different women he couldn't care for. He was an alcoholic, and he became very angry when he drank. I tried to get him help, but he was stubborn and would not get counseling. He eventually died from a brain aneurysm. I became depressed and felt like I had no one. My dad was supposed to be my hero, the one to provide, protect, and bring his children up in the discipline and instruction of the Lord.

Life was challenging, and I faced many obstacles. Despite all I had been through, I decided I would not quit. After graduating as a Medical Assistant, I sent over 100 resumes applying for work. I thought I had finally found my ideal job, as I was passionate about helping people. However, my husband, who was in the military, came home with the sad news that we were getting transferred, and I would have to move again. This would be our fourth move in 8 years. Living as a military spouse was very hard; I sometimes cried when I needed my husband, who was away serving the country. We never lived close to any relatives, so support was minimal. My children would visit my in-laws in New Jersey, allowing me to work and attend school. I enrolled in the nursing program and graduated as a licensed nurse. While working as a nurse, we bought our dream home; things were going well. I felt like I had finally bounced back through all the pain and hard times I faced.

Then came another sad news: my husband was transferring to work with the wounded warriors at Bethesda Military Hospital. I had to move, leaving my job, coworkers, family, and friends. I was so tired of moving that I begged my husband to let my son finish his last year of high school with his schoolmates and best friend. Being the new kid in high school can be very tough on a child. Moving to the DMV had its ups and downs, I never felt at home as I was missing Florida. Then life took another turn. Five years later, I experienced the most profound pain when my son became very ill and had no known diagnosis or etiology for his illness. The doctors told me to go and plan his funeral. My son contracted an unknown virus and was hospitalized; the doctors did several tests and could not find what was wrong with him. I saw my son falling into a coma before my very eyes.

I started praying and begging God not to take my son. One doctor told me to go home and prepare to bury my child. Once again, I became angry at the doctor, but a voice inside said that would not help my son. "Just go and pray." My Grandmother taught me not to fight the enemy in its comfort zone, I had to change my battleground and take my fight higher in the spiritual realm and let God take over my battle. With freezing temperatures and the worst snowstorms, my son was airlifted to Inova Heart Hospital. He had emergency surgery, and an Impella device was put in to assist his depressed heart function. My son's heart was failing. The doctors talked to us like they had no hope, but I had to stay positive. I now know whom to call on in my time of need.

My son was in ICU in a coma for ten days. I prayed over his body every second of the day. I would not leave his bedside. My family came to visit, we all held hands, prayed, and started singing over him. Shortly after, I saw one of his eyes open and close. I ran and called the nurse. The doctors told us our son was waking from the coma and they would remove the Impella device to see how he responded, when they took it out, all his vitals started dropping. The doctors immediately closed the door. I felt my heart pounding as my legs gave way, and I fell to the floor. When I gained consciousness, I went to the hospital chapel and collapsed on the floor. I don't know how long I was there, but I felt my husband shaking me to tell me the doctor was looking for me.

I rushed back to ICU only to hear that the device had cut two of my son's heart valves, and they needed to do emergency surgery, we had to decide on the type of replacement valve. A tissue valve or mechanical. This did not sound good, but after much research, I decided to go with the tissue valve. I started fasting and praying to God to save my son. The surgery went well, and my son was discharged home to continue occupational and Physical Therapy. It was challenging; thank God for returning my son to us. This showed me that I am strong and can survive anything with God by my side. Our bodies are a miracle, and we must care for ourselves. Life was unfair, and I had to learn early to forgive and deal with unfairness. It took a while to piece myself back together from the broken soul I was and all the challenges I had experienced.

It took one person (my aunt) who saw something in me to pull out what I had within me. The road to where I want to be will take time, patience, and fortitude. I gave my life to Christ and decided to follow His words. I overcame obstacles through my spiritual connection with God, self-love, meditation, and compassion. More decisive now, not afraid to take risks. I started a Children's charity called Kingdom Kids and started my own uniform scrub line. My husband and I purchased a villa in Jamaica called Restoration Villa where anyone can go and relax, rejuvenate, and restore what the enemy has stolen. I will not let the hurt of my past or life's twists and turns stop me from succeeding. I will continue to fight for my family; without them, I am nothing. I am the culmination of everything I've learned and experienced. Some beautiful, some painful, some horrific, but I am still standing, strong and proud.

Novellette Edwards Biography

Novellette Edwards is a wife, mother, and grandmother. I am a nurse pursuing a master's degree in public health at the University of Maryland Global Campus; my hobbies are reading, swimming, dancing, and listening to old-school music. I am the CEO of Sacred Heart Healthcare Agency; I am a founder and joint of Edwards Business Enterprise LLC. I am also the CEO of Essential Scrubs. These businesses help me to give back to several charities that I started and hope to one day open a shelter for abused women.

- Email: novnflorida@yahoo.com

Chapter 9:
A Purpose in Pain
By Rania Soliman

Many people appear to be functioning and leading seemingly normal lives, but behind closed doors are suffering in silence. Some struggle internally with navigating the unexpected challenges and pitfalls of everyday life while living in survival mode. Many frequently reflect on what possible choices they would have made in the past, had they had all the knowledge they currently have, not with regret, but in wonderment of how their life might have been. Recovering from childhood trauma is especially challenging when healing, while dealing with the very people who caused the trauma. Healing from either acute, chronic, or complex trauma is hard work, but much harder for those dealing with a combination. In cases when the parent is the abuser, continuing a relationship and interacting with them will likely retraumatize the child (young and old) and hinder their healing, keeping them in a dysregulated state.

When our past is our present, compassion and patience are vital, particularly when setting and keeping boundaries. Trying to balance this dynamic for many survivors is nearly impossible especially when simultaneously healing multiple past traumas. GOD created us women to experience more intense emotions in given areas of our body causing us to feel pain more severely than men. Our hormones play a huge role in our healing, therefore having our emotions acknowledged is of great value to us. Having said that, I would like to acknowledge you, especially if you grew up without a mother, or lost your mother, or miss your mother, or grieve the relationship you never had with your mother. Whoever you are, and wherever you are, I acknowledge you from a distance. Thankfully, GOD created us with an ability to change, to evolve developmentally, intellectually, and spiritually. In fact from the moment we exit our mother's womb we're constantly changing.

Innately curious beings with a desire to acquire knowledge and fascinated by origin stories. Naturally eager to explore and find purpose and are curious about childhood bonds. "GOD, grant us the serenity to accept the things we cannot change, the courage to change the things we can, and the wisdom to know the difference." (Psalm 27:10) The connection we have with our mothers is unique and unlike any other. Our family system shapes much of who we are, how we think of relationships, measure ambition and success, how we think of ourselves and how we regulate our emotions, our assumption of friends and strangers, and our relationship with GOD. Mothers are powerfully influential, even their attachment style (secure, anxious, avoidant, or disorganized) can impact how we show up in our adult relationships.

My quest for understanding my origin was after learning that neglect is the most common form of child abuse, followed by physical, verbal, emotional, religious, narcissistic, and sexual abuse. Adverse Childhood Experiences, a research study addressing potentially traumatizing experiences that can occur in childhood and adolescence validated my experiences. When I scored 6/10 my immediate concern was my children, hoping time would be on my side to break the cycle. Wondering if past ripples of attitudes, behaviors, and perceptions might have affected generations of women before me. Many women in past generations were deprived of support and suppressed their emotions, fearing judgment and shame. Perhaps women then had no choice but to tolerate more than we can endure now. Hopefully as the family dynamics continue to evolve from generation to generation, so will the parent and child dynamic. Many childhood trauma survivors struggle with carrying a heavy burden for decades, consumed with unhealed trauma trapped in their body.

Internally filled with grief, sadness, shame, guilt, anxiety, or anger. Some might battle with addiction, self-harm, or suicidal ideation.

Many question their faith in GOD, and with nothing to compare their experiences against, their actions and behaviors are their only reality. Subsequently, many children are blamed, ridiculed, and scapegoated, ultimately traumatized at no fault of their own. It's unfortunate that the very people we depend on for protection and support can significantly dismiss and violate our trust and well-being. That was my reality for many years, compelling me to make sense of and understand the long term impact my childhood experiences had on me all these years. Eager to understand my relationship with GOD, since HE was present in my ruminating thoughts. It became clear to me that one of the root causes or dilemmas that influence how children view GOD during challenging experiences had actually nothing to do with GOD. It was rather the people with rigid religious beliefs, and their endless shaming deeming children sinful for life.

Many had no choice but to disaffiliate from any religious practices and activities. Some denounced their faith altogether, feeling judged and ridiculed must mean that GOD also thinks that of them. Like many Trauma-Informed Educators and Healing Professionals, my personal story in the trauma space began with my own experiences. Growing up with no foundation and understanding of Islam left me clueless about GOD. Growing up in Egypt, my experiences were my only reality. I wasn't an unhappy child, but I was a very lonely child. Being exposed to certain behaviors left me curious about things I had no business being curious about. My parents did their best, they were physically present but emotionally disengaged. They provided for my basic needs like food, shelter, clothing, and education, which I'm grateful for. My mother's rules became rigid, her discipline was physical and stern, often justified as tough love.

It saddens me, looking back, that perhaps she experienced something traumatic in her childhood that profoundly affected her to end up the way she did. But that doesn't excuse her actions and behaviors. Being an authoritarian mother with extreme narcissistic traits remains to be what keeps us apart decades later. My father, on the other hand, was the peacekeeper, the dreamer, adventurous and humorous, making it easier to gravitate more towards him. Moving to the US was the beginning of many events that later destroyed our family unit. Moving was exciting, but like most immigrant children, I struggled adjusting to the culture and environment my first year like any typical 10-year-old. But my world officially turned upside down within a few years. I experienced parental separation and divorce shortly after my father left us.

The event leading up to that is when the suicidal attempts started. Losing my father changed the dynamic at home with my mother. Within months, being at home felt like a war zone on enemy territory, and I was the only hostage, captured and tortured. A funny analogy now, but an endless nightmare then, especially when dodging bullets in the form of emotional, verbal, and physical abuse. Despite my reality then, the worst was yet to come, that one defining experience that fundamentally changed me. Betrayal! For approximately 3 years, I was sexually molested, groomed and manipulated. The events leading up to that experience were confusing to comprehend back then. I struggled with two ongoing thoughts then, if my father never left it wouldn't have happened, and if my mother didn't leave me unsupervised it wouldn't have happened.

What that man did wasn't what destroyed my sense of self-worth, it was my mother not protecting me, before, during, and after that destroyed me and influenced my life choices well into my adulthood. Experiencing suicidal ideation consumed me until my 9th grade teacher learned about my ongoing suicidal attempts. She contacted child protective services, and being hospitalized for several months to get help and support was the only solution then. Being discharged months later meant going back home would be my reality again. Despite my experiences, I continued to be silent about the sexual abuse. That part of my life also got buried away and was never to be talked about again once my mother found out. The rejection and betrayal wounds were officially born that year. The embarrassment and inconvenience I caused my mother became a burden which granted me the role of the family scapegoat.

By 11th grade, child protective services approved for me to temporarily reside with a friend and her family. It was then I attended a church service for the first time and experienced a glimpse of hope. Moving back home was inevitable, which meant more broken promises. As the abuse increased, so did my anger, and I fought back. My attempt to protect myself led to calling 911 to teach me a lesson on fighting back. Being handcuffed, shoved in a cop car like a mischievous troubled teenager felt like I was outside of my body looking in on me. Thankfully, my guidance counselor requested that my case be reviewed, hoping the judge will have the real facts and approve my transfer to live temporarily in a youth shelter. My transfer was granted, and I lived there for several months.

Being released by my 18th birthday meant that going back would be my reality again. A part of me hoped everything would be better this time, but within weeks, I moved out. Working full time wasn't enough to live and survive on my own. Thankfully my friend and her family invited me to live with them again, which meant church was an option again. One random Sunday, the pastor shared, "When my father and my mother forsake me, then the LORD will take me up." (Psalm

27:10) Hearing that was cathartic and my desire for more knowledge about Christianity increased. Meeting my first husband at church felt like GOD was somehow rewarding me. Becoming a mother shortly after gave me hope, made me feel loved by GOD.

But sadness visited me again when my son Jameel got diagnosed with leukodystrophy, an incurable disease with a one-year life expectancy, ending his young life right before his first birthday. Grieving his loss and the concept of death at the time wasn't anything I had experienced or witnessed before. Holding my son and hearing him take his last breath was an experience I can't articulate or explain, even now it's still hard to explain. My 20-year-old self, at the time, struggled internally. The stages of grief were unfamiliar, leaving me confused with all my emotions. My coping choices back then destroyed my marriage and overnight, I had lost my son, my husband, myself, and eventually my connection with GOD.

Looking back, I was detached from my body and severely dysregulated. Barely surviving emotionally, wanting to blend in as I struggled to keep my head above water was my only option then. Much of my mood in my 20s was based on what was happening in my personal and professional life. Looking back, I dissociated and disconnected from my feelings and memories, distracting myself with just about anything to avoid my feelings was my reality. This resulted in making poor life choices and engaging in extremely toxic relationships. My therapists didn't speak about how trauma impacts the body or how to regulate my nervous system or how to manage my emotions. I had no knowledge then of the body, heart, and mind connection, and I stayed in a cycle of survival until my early 40s wondering what was wrong with me.

My desire for change seemed impossible and as my children got older my choice of parenting style was foreign and unfamiliar because it was never modeled in my childhood.

Divorcing their father made it hard on them to cope with having their parents be apart. The hardest part was simultaneously reparenting myself while parenting my 3 children. I feared repeating history and was frequently hypervigilant, leaving me extremely exhausted. After hitting one of the absolute lowest points in my life, I thought about my children and the life they deserve. I realized quickly that something drastic needed to change. GOD chose the healing path for me, and my main priority was to show up for them, the way the younger me deserved to have her mother show up for her.

Thankfully now they have shown me how resilient they are; having them was the best aspect of my life because it was them getting older and forming their own personality that ultimately empowered me to keep healing. My relationship with GOD slowly transformed (still a work in progress) my entire perspective and outlook on life. I felt like I was sleeping all those years and GOD finally woke up. My belief in GOD meant to fully trust HIM and stop doubting HIS love for me. I invited GOD permanently in my life and stopped fearing the unknown. Like many survivors, I felt discouraged at first, unaware of how uncomfortable, messy, and scary healing would be. But those who dare to welcome change in their life, unknowingly welcome hope which creates space for faith, endless possibilities, renewal and transformation.

I remember hearing once that people change for 4 reasons, they've been hurt enough they have to, they've learned enough they want to, they've seen enough they're inspired to, or they've received enough they're able to. I found comfort in believing that GOD is omniscient, and HE knows all that there is to know and all that can be known. HE is the creator of all things. HE is aware of the past, present, and future and nothing takes HIM by surprise. HIS knowledge is total, therefore our journey here on earth is preordained. This was a turning point in my life as I accepted that while my past was incredibly painful, it also had power and purpose, which naturally manifested when I welcomed change and healing in my life.

So for all you "SURVIVORS"; you "CYCLE BREAKERS"; and you "TRUTH SEEKERS" out there, be grateful that GOD chose the healing path for you. Hopefully you think non-defensively about who you are (in small ways and large) despite whatever your distant past might have contributed to who you became, and who you are now. My quest for healing and understanding my trauma wasn't about what actually happened to me, it was more about what happened inside of me as a result of what happened to me. My choice to honor my inner child is to have clear boundaries that give me strength and patience to interact with my parents in small doses. I chose to be distant, but close enough to allow space within me to have compassion and empathy for my parents so I can sincerely pray for them.

I'm grateful that GOD had much bigger plans than I had for myself. My healing cycle went from hope, renewal to transformation. My biggest obstacles turned out to be my biggest opportunities, allowing me to show up for myself, my children, and my clients. Every experience in my life was to lead me to where I am today. My new set of beliefs, attitudes, hopes, and values keep me going until my soul returns to its place of origin, with my creator in heaven.
"We belong to GOD and to Him we shall Return." (Qur'an 2:156)

Rania Soliman Biography

Like many Trauma-Informed Professionals and Practitioners, Rania Soliman's experience in the trauma space began with her own healing and lifelong recovery journey. Rania's path to healing was rooted in compassionately understanding the imprints of trauma and the impact of adverse childhood experiences. Through healing, she regained the parts of her that were lost for decades. GOD transformed Rania's pain into purpose, HE turned her obstacles into opportunities, and gave her strength to show up more for herself, her children, and her clients. Experiencing the power of somatic practices taught her to be more present with her body and regulate her nervous system. Rania's quest for healing allowed her to share the knowledge and resources she wishes she could have had years ago, to the space of supporting others to feel seen, heard, valued and less alone on their healing journey.

- Email: coachingwithrania@gmail.com
- Website: www.raniasoliman.com/

Chapter 10:
The Final Run
By Mavis H. Bubb

There are no losses, just lessons

Do painful lessons cause you to go deep within to make life-changing decisions? Do challenging experiences cause you to peel back the mask and reveal the real you? Do adverse circumstances put you in a fight or flight mode? Recently I stumbled across this quote by Les Brown: "The good times we put in our pocket, the bad times we put in our heart." What an insight! I still carry the lessons learned from the bad times deep within my heart. I still think about the difficult lessons and experiences that resulted in major turning points in my life. Looking back, had it not been for that resilient spirit instilled in me from an early age I would not have been able to rise from my seasons of pain and flight to continue to fight.

Growing up in a Christian home with my parents and five siblings on the tiny island of Grenada, after leaving my homeland St. Vincent, was the beginning of an interesting journey. Things were tough financially. My dad was the pastor of a small community church and my mom who had left her teaching job to take care of us, supported my dad full time in the ministry. Consequently, I had to learn to be content with the little my parents could have afforded us. No matter how tough it was, my parents always emphasized the importance of having a good education. They made several sacrifices to ensure my siblings and I had all we needed for school. Our attendance record was impeccable! Even more important was our spiritual development. They taught us the importance of developing a personal relationship with God through prayer, reading the Bible and attending church regularly. This led me to give my heart to Christ at the age of 12. Because of this upbringing I developed a resilience which prepared me for what I would face later in life.

As any young person, I had my ups and downs. But I remained steadfast in my faith and was very involved in church activities. I truly enjoyed the things of God. I longed for the day when I would grow up, get married and have a loving family of my own. So, you can imagine how happy I was when, years later, I got married to a man of God who had Christian values and principles and who vowed to love and take care of me. Walking down the aisle of that church with my dad on that lovely Saturday evening in a beautiful ceremony among pastors, family, and friends was a dream come true. Surely, this was the beginning of a wonderful life, or so I thought.

My Affliction
The first two years of my marriage were great. During that time, my first son was born. I was ecstatic. Given my upbringing, my husband and I both vowed to raise him in the fear of the Lord. Despite my new-found bundle of joy, trouble started brewing in the marriage. Four months after my son was born, much to my chagrin I had to return to work. As you can well imagine, it was tough for my husband and me, but I wanted to because I had moved through the ranks very quickly in my organization to senior supervisor within 10 years; a rare achievement I did not take lightly.

My husband, however, demanded that I remain at home to take care of my son as according to him, this was my role as a mother and wife. I was completely taken aback as we never agreed to this before we got married. Nowhere in my wildest dreams had I ever considered leaving my job at the peak of my banking career. I wanted to be a wife and a mother, but I also wanted my career. I know that this may sound selfish. It was as if I was putting my career over my marriage and raising my son. But the real issue for me here was that I felt I was losing my freedom. The manner in which my husband communicated this to me made me feel trapped. I did not sign up for this.

In addition, I did not feel this was the will of God for me, so I prayed night and day for God to change my husband's heart. It felt like my husband was not taking me seriously and since I needed to get back to work within a month, I decided to take matters into my own hands. I left home for a few days without telling anyone so that I could further seek the face of God. I took my son with me On my return, my husband apologized, and we found a competent babysitter that provided the comfort for me to return to work.

On The Run
Needless to say, my husband's change of heart was short-lived. He began expressing reservations about 'strangers' in the home. It was clear he did not want a babysitter taking care of his child and things began to get ugly in the relationship, emotionally and mentally. At this point, my job and my marriage were on the line.

Because of my Christian upbringing and fear of divorce, I resigned from my job two months after returning to work rationalizing that after 12 years of committed and dedicated service to the bank, it was the time to leave. I do not recall praying intensely about this decision as I felt I had this under control and things would improve. But I was wrong. The emotional and mental abuse returned like cancer but this time it was worse because the abuse also became physical, and this physical abuse occurred while I was pregnant with my second son. Things got so bad, that like Mary the mother of Jesus, I fled for my safety, the safety of my son and my unborn child. I found safety in my parents' home, solace in reading the scriptures, praying, and attending church regularly. Some months later, my husband convinced me that he had a change of heart. He apologized and asked for my forgiveness. Again, my compassionate heart took over. I forgave him and went back to being with him.

After the birth of my second son, emotional abuse raised its ugly head again. We received counselling from our Pastor on more than one occasion. Nevertheless, the abuse, intense pain and hurt continued, forcing me to leave home yet another time with my sons. During that time, God opened the door for me to return to the same bank on a contractual basis. Even though I was now employed, as a single mom my salary was not adequate to support myself and my two sons and I needed help. Therefore, I was more than grateful when my husband decided to provide some support. Though we were still separated, our communication began to improve, and I noticed what appeared to be positive signs of genuine change. I picked up the broken pieces of my life and made yet another attempt at reuniting.

The relationship went well for a while, and I felt our marriage was on the road to recovery. However, that recovery was short-lived. Within a few months, emotional abuse set in, and things took a turn for the worse. I felt betrayed, deceived, and deeply hurt. However, I never once questioned my faith in God. My sons were older now and were very much aware of the tension in the home. It was during this time my son, who was ten, asked a simple and powerful question that would change the rest of my life. Looking at me sadly one day he asked, "Mom, why did you come back?" That question pierced through my heart like a dagger. The thought of having my sons grow up in an unstable and unhealthy environment was way too painful. Collecting my thoughts, I slowly responded, "I thought things had changed and were going to be better." While I did not mention anything further to my son at that point, it became clear to me that I could not continue living a runaway life. Like Esther in the Bible who risked her life and went into the King uninvited, in order to save her people, I too had to take urgent action to save the 3 Ss of my life – Sons, Self and Sanity.

The Turning Point
John Maxwell said, "A bend in the road is not the end of the road unless you fail to make the turn." Well, that day, I got the courage to make that life-changing turn and took my final run from that abusive twelve-year marriage. During my ordeal, I

was too ashamed and embarrassed to let anyone know what was happening to me. As a matter of fact, based on my belief system, I felt that I had to live up to social, cultural, and religious expectations of being a good wife. After all, I was a believer and raised in a Christian home. What would people say if I left? How would my parents feel? Making that turn in my life allowed me to find myself again. I was no longer afraid and ashamed of what others would say. I was finally free!

Rising From the Ashes

What was it that brought me to the place where I was no longer afraid of what others would say? As I alluded to earlier, throughout this entire ordeal it was the tenants of my faith, the Holy Spirit and prayer and the values I held dearly that enabled me to rise from life's adversities to embrace and leverage opportunities presented to me.

God said in His Word that He will restore what the caterpillar and cankerworm have eaten (Joel 2:25). And He certainly did that for me. Within 12 years, I rose from the ashes of unemployment to employment; from temporary contract status to the permanent position of senior supervisor and shortly thereafter to the rank of senior management. My rapid progression within the organization was faster than in my first twelve years! Had it not been for my resilient faith and God's intervention, my growth may not have advanced to where it is today. Like Job, God began to restore and strengthen me with the resilience to courageously face the vicissitudes of life. It was that resilience I leaned on to take leaps of faith and experience God in miraculous ways in my life and the lives of my children.

God provided scholarships for me to pursue a master's degree; scholarships for my sons to attend university; a brand-new vehicle within 4 months of selling my vehicle and resorting to public transportation and He is still moving in my life up to today. I can truly say I have risen from the ashes of divorce to enjoying an abundant life in Christ.

According to Warren G. Lester, "Success in life comes not from holding a good hand, but in playing a poor hand well." It may appear that life dealt me a poor hand and I could have wallowed in the mire. Today, however, I reflect with gratitude on the transformation, resilience, hope and renewal that took place in my life. I wish to share the lessons learned with you with the hope that you will be inspired to respond appropriately to your own challenges and seasons of pain.

Reflecting With Gratitude

1. Maintain a positive attitude in adversity

What stance do you adopt when you are going through a painful experience? Do you ask God "why me?" Do you say life has dealt you an unfair blow and wallow in self-pity? I know that remaining positive in pain can be difficult. Nevertheless, Joseph in the Old Testament chose to remain positive in the face of false accusation and God promoted him from prison to palace. The resilience I developed in my adversity came first from my faith and trust in God and then from the support of family and my spiritual leaders. I did not know how, or when, but I remained positive knowing that one day God was going to get me out of that rut I had found myself in. And He did!

2. Find the lesson in difficult experiences

No matter what adversity you have gone through in life, you have the opportunity to learn and grow. In her book *Live Your Life from The Inside Out,* Dr. Maureen McIntosh Alberts speaks about the importance of learning lessons from life's challenges such that they leave you better and not bitter. I chose to become better; I chose to stop recreating myself into someone else and appreciate and value myself. God made each of us uniquely in His image and likeness for His honor and glory and we deserve the best. No matter what situation you are going through, learn from the experience and be willing to search for the lesson until you find it.

3. Find your purpose and start living it

How many people have failed to fulfill their God-given potential because of the knocks of life or because of fear of the unknown? The experiences from my pain fueled my passion to become a Certified Leadership Coach to help leaders connect with their purpose and create transformation in their lives. You too can find purpose in your pain and begin that journey of transformation today.

4. Take care of you – you cannot give what you do not have

According to Dr. Maureen Mc Intosh Alberts, "Life does not give you what you want, life gives you who you are." Taking care of your spiritual, emotional, and physical well-being are of paramount importance. An air hostess, giving instruction before the aircraft takes off, reminds passengers to put on their life jacket first before attempting to save anyone else. The same holds true for you and the people in your life. Fill yourself first and then you will be able to give to others. I continue to take care of myself in all the dimensions of my life so I can give to others. I have not arrived; I continue to grow and learn daily.

Undoubtedly, my series of afflictions drew me closer to God and gave me a testimony to share with the world. I would say the adversity I suffered worked together for my good (Rom 8:28). The Apostle Paul encourages us in Romans 8:18 to consider afflictions as nothing compared with the glory we shall receive in the end. The glory I received is finding my life purpose in the adversity I went through which I am now living. You too can find your life's purpose in adversity and pain.

Mavis H. Bubb Biography

Mavis H. Bubb is a Maxwell Certified Leadership Coach, Trainer and Speaker who has overcome many life challenges on her way to becoming a successful senior career banker. Her resilience and insatiable appetite for personal growth and development inspired her to launch her leadership coaching career in 2021 to help leaders connect with their purpose, create new results, and transform their lives. As a Leadership Coach, she provides structure and accountability to enable her clients to accelerate their personal growth and success. She is a sought-after presenter and speaker and has facilitated workshops and group coaching sessions across several businesses and organizations like Republic Bank and Cable and Wireless. Mavis is also a person of faith and currently serves on the Leadership Team at the Evangelistic Centre in Grenada. Her mantra in life is, "If something is worth doing, it's worth doing well."

- Email: coaching@mavisbubb.com
- Facebook: www.facebook.com/mavismcburnie
- Instagram: www.instagram.com/mav_hannah/
- LinkedIn: www.linkedin.com/in/mavismcburnie/

Chapter 11:
Finding Understanding While Persevering Through Pain
By Dr. Catherine Pearson

In the depths of hopelessness, we often seek solace and healing in unexpected ways. We look for signs of divine intervention to guide us through our darkest moments, inspired by stories of God sending angels in human form to rescue us. In my journey, I unexpectedly encountered not one but two car accidents within a mere three weeks, altering the course of my life. This chapter is a testament to the power of faith, resilience, and the Holy Spirit to find understanding and healing in the face of adversity.

Life Turned Upside Down
Have you ever found yourself standing on unshakable faith, consistently praying, immersing yourself in God's promises daily, living and leading righteously, and firmly believing in God for supernatural outcomes? One moment, you feel like you are on top of the world, alive and fulfilled with God's strength, and the next, you find yourself plummeting into the emptiness of deep depression, desperately clinging to hope in pain. That's precisely how I felt after two traumatic car accidents temporarily altered the course of my life within the short span of three weeks.

In the first accident, a reckless driver slammed into the back of my car, sandwiching me between two vehicles on a congested highway. The incomprehensible trauma left me delusional, shaken, battered, and in excruciating pain. After being discharged from the emergency room, I was deeply wounded and unable to drive. As I recovered, I had little confidence to drive. Fear limited my commutes to very short distances for necessities. I made a conscious effort to steer clear of the highways, even when it required me to travel double the time to get to appointments. Little did I know that this season marked the beginning of an exacerbating journey.

Less than three weeks later, I found myself confronting a twist of fate. As I persisted in minimizing my travel time and trying to avoid the main highways, a drunk driver, numbed by alcohol, plowed into my car recklessly. He callously fled the scene, leaving me desolated from a second accident that further devastated my life. In the wake of the collision, I was filled with anger, fear, trauma, and helplessness. Then Jonah mysteriously appeared on the highway and comforted me with assurance as we waited for help. Moments later, Isaiah arrived with compelling news that he followed the driver until he surrendered to the police. With biblical names, I thought God was sending His Angels to minister to me.

Shortly after, my physical and mental health had been thrust into a disruptive storm -struggling to take a few steps and feeling radiating pain from torn muscles and herniated discs. I felt as though a brain injury completely turned my entire world upside down. While combatting memory loss, I had relentless spells of nausea, debilitating dizziness, sleepless nights, pulsating migraines that refused to relent, and a pervasive sense of confusion that obstructed my mind. My doctor instructed me only to sleep and remain motionless whenever I was awake. It was as if I were trapped in a disorienting entanglement, unable to find my way back to the life I once knew.

Obsessed with Journaling
After these traumatic accidents, I morphed into an all-consuming obsession with journaling. Suffering from memory loss and fearing I would forget, I journaled as my lifeline. I felt that my only responsibility now was to meticulously document my existence as if my identity depended on it. I

wondered if this was all life had in store for me—an unremitting pursuit of the intricacies of my existence. I made the difficult decision to step back from the demands of daily life. I realized that this was not the life I wanted. I refused to allow journaling to become my entire existence, overshadowing the other facets of my recovery. Therefore, I embarked on the arduous journey of reclaiming my life and rediscovering my identity, one step at a time.

Memory Loss and Frustration
Reclaiming my life consisted of slowly dressing in my best fashions daily, jewelry, and other accessories. As I tentatively reentered the realm of the living, I soon discovered that interaction with others had become an exercise in frustration. The more I engaged with people, the more elusive my memories became. Dates, names, faces, and even the identities of cherished family members seemed to dissolve into an impenetrable fog, which frustrated me. The frustration led to recurring headaches. I also struggled with sensitivity to brightness, adding another layer of distress. Bright lights triggered a cascade of pain that would persist for days or weeks. The headaches would stealthily creep into my consciousness, starting as a dull ache before radiating to different areas, engulfing my concentration in agonizing pain.

To make matters worse, I noticed that even the simplest task had become an exercise in futility. I could begin a task in one room only to find myself in another without recollection of what I had set out to accomplish. The frustration and confusion were relentless, and I grew weary of attempting to explain my plight to others. Even the simplest tasks had become formidable challenges. I could no longer remember how to prepare my favorite dish, lasagna, which I prepared countless times and always devoured with joy. The world had suddenly become alienated, and I felt like a foreigner. Even my neighbor, whom I had known very well, I embarrassingly could not recall his name. I was experiencing detached emotions from my family and friends. The most heartbreaking moment was discovering my loss of passion to continue to serve in the business God divinely appointed. I was uncertain and cried out, "God, You called me to serve! Only You God!" I consistently prayed in the Spirit and listened to sermons and spiritual music.

God reminded me that He's always my lifeline. God spoke to me in dreams and visions. To name a few: an invisible floor, two sets of legs, and me dissipating from a photo. Late at night, I had a divine encounter with God. He spoke to me, answering my prayers and revealing the meaning of the dreams and visions. God said, "I detached your feelings because the very thing I sent you to serve became your idol- your intense passion and love for people. The invisible floor symbolized that I was carrying you. The two sets of legs depicted your attempts to take control. The photo represented the seasons when certain assignments ended, but you extended the season by being distracted and serving unaligned with My Will."

A Battle Living a Different Life
With each passing day, I became acutely aware of my irritability. I struggled to contain it. I fought to maintain composure to respond with kindness and patience. However, I often found myself short-tempered, speaking sternly and occasionally raising my voice—a far cry from the person I once was.

This internal turmoil led to an overwhelming desire to spend more quiet time with God. In solitude, I could escape the expectations and judgments of others, freeing myself from the need to explain or justify my altered state. While those around me held on to their expectations of who I should be, I contended with the harsh reality that I was now living a different life—a life defined by adaptability, survival, and the relentless battle to make it through each day.

Turning to Faith
As a devout Christian, my faith has always been an unshakable foundation in my life. God was always the Rock upon which I had built my beliefs, hopes, and dreams. While navigating challenging opportunities through this journey filled with pain, confusion, and frustration, my faith endured its most profound examination. Life had taken an unexpected turn, and all I had left to lean on was my faith in God. In moments of weakness and doubt, God's Word became my refuge when the enemy threatened to steal my hope. His Promises of His unfailing love and steadfast presence provided the light where I once suffocated in darkness.

God said, "I will never leave you nor forsake you," His Word declared, and that assurance was enough to sustain me. In the midst of a devastating emotional breakdown, I found myself alone at home, crying uncontrollably, struggling to maintain my faith. I pushed myself to engage in praise and worship to God, desperate for some semblance of solace. During this vulnerable moment, my phone rang, and a beautiful, reassuring voice spoke. Someone I knew and trusted whispered comforting words affirming God was with me. I was not alone in my struggles.

Learning to Accept Help
I hadn't realized that I needed help until the fragile façade of normalcy I had constructed suddenly fell apart again. The brain injury caused so much confusion that I remained oblivious to my need for help. Consequently, I didn't know to ask. Little did I know that God would use phone calls to make me realize the need to seek assistance. This time, I received a second phone call from a Grace Church Family member inquiring about my health and whether I needed help. In my confused state, I responded that I was in pain, and I asked about her upcoming trip. She gently reminded me that she had already returned, an unsettling indication of the depth of my disorientation.

Thereafter, members of my Grace Church Family, other ministries, and friends showered me with love. He reaffirmed with reflections of Jonah, Isaiah, and Emmanuelle, an Uber driver who committed to driving me around. God helped me realize my burdens were too great to bear alone. I was deeply grateful for everyone's intervention.

Believing for Healing
Interventions became a testament to the extraordinary healing power of faith. During this time, I understood a fundamental truth—pain serves a purpose. In the past, I often prayed for suffering to end and my pain to cease. Instead, I prayed for the strength to endure, the patience to persevere, and the unwavering trust in God to see me through even when the reasons behind my suffering remain a mystery.

God's power was always at my disposal, waiting for me to exercise my faith and receive the victory He had already won for me. This healing period brought profound moments— moments when I witnessed the supernatural healing of my shoulder as I prayed for rest and sweet sleep. Then God called me to pray more and more, return to church, and only serve in the prayer ministry. As I prayed for people at the altar during Sunday services, I surprisingly did not need my glasses to mask the glare of light. Eventually, my neck and back pain subsided from the herniated discs. I continued to pray and stand in unwavering faith—no more piercing headaches. Praise and worship became sweet music that captivated my soul as I danced with Jesus in the sanctuary.

Lessons in Perseverance
Life's disruptions are like unexpected storms that can leave us battered and broken. In those moments of turmoil, I found myself questioning the purpose of my pain. We may wonder why God has allowed us to endure such trials. I tapped into the immense power God had already bestowed upon me to

persevere through life's most challenging tribulations, even when I did not fully understand the reasons behind my suffering.

1. **The Purpose in Pain:** Pain is not always a curse but can serve a greater purpose. Sometimes, we should pray not for the end of our suffering but for the strength to endure it and the patience to trust in God's plan, even when we do not understand. In these moments, we need to remember 1 Peter 5:10 NLT. "So after you have suffered a little while, He will restore, support, and strengthen you, and He will place you on a firm foundation." Galatians 2:20 NLT: "I have been crucified with Christ, and I no longer live, but Christ lives in me. The life I now live in the body, I live by faith in the Son of God, who loved me and gave Himself for me."
2. **Blindly Trusting God:** We find ourselves in situations opposing God's Will. Sometimes, we must trust God unquestioningly, allowing Him to lead us even when we cannot see the path with our natural eyes. We must use His light rather than relying solely on our limited understanding. An invisible floor exemplified God carrying me. He is still present right beside us, with provisions and abundant resources already available. God doesn't rely on us to guide His course for our lives. God said to me, "My way, not your way. I prepared the path for you."
3. **Whole-Hearted Devotion:** God desires our whole-hearted devotion and trust. He wants us to place our complete faith in Him, knowing that He alone can guide, empower, enlighten, and direct our lives with His perfect wisdom, power, knowledge, and understanding. In Matthew 22:34-37 NLT, Jesus emphasizes this whole-hearted devotion: You must love the Lord your God with all your heart, all your soul, and all your mind."

Emerging After the Storm
I learned from my experience that life's fate is no coincidence. My transformation began here. I gained infinite wisdom and insight birthed from my journey through the complexities of recovery and internal spiritual battles impacted by two life-altering accidents. I've walked the path from pain to purpose, and I'm here to walk the path with others. My memory loss, physical pain, and emotional affliction have deepened my capacity for empathy and ignited an insatiable desire to connect with women. As a Life Coach, I help them to recognize and intensively break through barriers to manifest and walk in true freedom.

Amid unimaginable pain, God's presence became my solace. He wept with me, offering the empathy of a friend who needed no words or solutions. Sometimes, all we need is to sit in His presence, to just be and feel His profound understanding. Life unfolds in seasons, each with its unique purpose. We must learn to listen to the whispers of The Holy Spirit and recognize when a season has ended. Sometimes, we pray for sickness to end when we should instead pray for the strength to carry us through, the patience to endure, and the trust to know that God's plan, though mysterious, is always for our good.

God doesn't always heal us all at once. His healing touch extends beyond physical ailments to the depths of our emotional wounds, manifesting His healing and making us whole. In the words of Romans 8:28, we find solace in knowing that all things work together for good for those who love God and are called according to His purpose. Philippians 4:13 NKJV, "I can do all things through Christ who strengthens me." remains a sign of hope and a testament to steadfast faith.

Dr. Catherine Pearson Biography

Dr. Catherine Pearson, CEO of Emergent Consulting Solutions, LLC., leverages 20+ years of executive-level expertise in business and professional development. As a decorated Army Veteran, she excels in improvement studies and sustainable practices for global and domestic initiatives. Her career highlights yielding 10% operational efficiency gains and orchestrating the seamless transition of 10,000+ personnel into new healthcare facilities. Dr. Pearson's innovation extends to budget management, achieving cost savings of up to $3 million. She also mentored Career Consultants, leading to a 6% increase in student selection rates and securing an additional $1.7 million for healthcare programs. A devoted advocate for Veterans, she facilitates the military-to-civilian career transition. Dr. Pearson drives communal change and supports charitable causes, helping raise over $750K. Dr. Pearson holds a Doctorate in Business Administration and certifications as a Professional Coach. She is committed to mediation, diversity, equity, and inclusion.

- Email: emergentconsultingsolutions@gmail.com
- Website: www.emergentconsultingsolutions.com

Chapter 12:
The Power of Anchoring on Faith, Truth, Passion, and Purpose
By Ilka V. Wilson

"Trust the process of pain. Anchor on your faith, the truth, your passion, and your purpose."
– ILKA V. WILSON VALLEE

Psalm 61:2 (ESV) - "From the end of the earth I call to you when my heart is faint. Lead me to the rock that is higher than I." Pain is a natural part of life that everyone experiences at one point or another. The feeling of pain can come in many forms such as physical, emotional, mental, and spiritual. Pain can be the result of various human experiences such as loss, grief, betrayal, abuse, divorce, and failure. The feeling of pain is unpleasant, and no one wants to experience it. However, pain can also teach valuable lessons, and when dealt with in the right way, it can be transformed into a purpose-driven life. "To realize the worth of the anchor we need to feel the storm." - Corrie ten Boom.

In 2014, I was diagnosed with a very rare form of cancer (a GIST-gastrointestinal stromal tumor). In 2015, I was in chemotherapy to treat the tumor post operation, my husband decided our marriage was over and he was moving out to, in his words, "Pursue his happiness." And I began questioning my choice of vocation. I felt lost, hurt, and confused, as though I was falling to the bottom of the ocean and there was no ocean floor. How could a "good person" be faced with so much hurt? Someone who only tried to be kind, helpful, and loving, go through all of this at once? I could not make sense of this season. I felt as though God had come to my table and cleared everything off the table...flipping my table over in anger. Yes, this was a major season of pain for me.

I contemplated the reality that my health, family, and career was in jeopardy. I, however, questioned if it was really in jeopardy or was God clearing everything I relied on so I could rely on Him? You will see in the lessons to follow that God sometimes takes us on a difficult journey, that sometimes makes no sense, to re-route us to our God-aligned purpose. Experiencing deep pain coupled with watching my children experience the same or a deeper pain triggered me to make critical decisions. Decisions such as, do I remain stuck and hold on to the pain and hurt or do I keep moving forward until the pain subsides? Do I ignore my values and do like the world expects or do I anchor in my values, my faith, and the truth? Do I pursue my purpose and passion or just settle because I faced a bad break? Do I find ways to transform my pain to purpose and inspiration or remain bitter, discontented, and toxic?

As a mom, these are just a few of the many questions that required a decision during a season of major life trials in my health, family relationships, and my vocation. Despite the deep pain, I reached a fork in the road where I asked myself, 'Will you allow this pain to kill you or will it strengthen you? Will you take the wide road and do what the world prescribes a.k.a. do what everyone is expecting? Or will you take the road less traveled, the hard and high road?' Deciding to anchor on faith, truth, and purpose, no matter how deep the pain I was experiencing was a decision I made in 2016. That no matter how low the valley and darkness of the road, I must persevere and continue to do the right thing, make the right choices, for the right reason.

I realized that life experiences are gifts sent to fulfill a greater purpose that are not immediately understood. Transforming pain to purpose is a journey that begins when one chooses to learn from their pain rather than run away from it. It is not always easy to transform pain into a purpose-driven life, but it is possible with commitment, honesty, and determination. In deciding what will anchor you, truth or lie, pain or purpose. In this chapter, I share seven steps on how deciding to anchor in my truth and faith transformed my pain to purpose.

Step One: Acknowledge the Pain. The first step in transforming pain to purpose is acknowledging the pain. Pain can be a difficult emotion to deal with, and many people choose to avoid it or bury it deep down in their subconscious. However, when we do this, we are only prolonging the healing process, and it may come back and cause more harm in the future. Therefore, it is essential to acknowledge the pain and own your part, and work through the process. Running from the pain, tucking it away, or deciding to create a fantasy life to mask the pain does no good. I learned during this phase that to acknowledge the pain I needed to take time and sit with myself. Through a gift from my doctor who told me that I "needed to decide" as my health condition was not improving. When I was told to take time off (3 months) to decide, what I heard was this was a critical decision for me. A decision whether I would choose life or death. That I could not continue to fight for my health, marriage, and vocation all at the same time. It could be the death of me.

This time allowed me the margin to identify the type of pain I felt and the source of the pain. I had to accept that pain was part of my reality in that season of my life. It helped me sift through and better understand what triggered the pain. I began to understand then that acknowledging the pain was not about self-blaming, it was about taking responsibility for your own emotions and allowing yourself to feel them fully. "Pain signals resetting and transformation on the way."

Step Two: Face the Pain. After I acknowledged the pain and understood that being "superwoman" was not a choice, I then had to face the pain. This means accepting that pain exists. Facing pain can be challenging, especially if the pain is deep-rooted and was ignored for a long time. However, it's a necessary step in transforming pain to purpose. In standing firm in your truth, as it allows you to confront the emotions surrounding the pain. I had to be honest with myself, my current reality, and how I felt. This meant expressing my emotions and thoughts without fear of judgment. Writing was cathartic for me (something I learned during this season of deep pain.) Journaling the pain and lessons learned, as I learned it and lived it, led me to my launch as an author in 2016 in my first collaboration book, *Success University for Women in Business*, where I wrote about one of the first lessons in this journey of deep pain, "Honor Your Values."

Journaling is just one way to face the pain. Another way to face your pain is to seek out wise and "truth speaking" friends, therapists, or a medical professional for guidance and support. What worked for me was prayer, connecting with God and reading the truth from the Bible along with therapy. I learned during this step that when you face pain, you allow yourself to be vulnerable, and vulnerability leads to healing. I now understand that facing the pain was the beginning of my decision to start the healing process not knowing how long it would take. Remember, feeling the pain doesn't mean you will be destroyed. It allows you to begin the healing process. You cannot heal what you don't feel, face, or embrace.

Step Three: Embrace the Pain. Embracing the pain means accepting it as part of your life and learning from it. Pain can teach us valuable lessons about ourselves, our relationships, and our purpose in life. When we embrace pain, we begin to see it as an opportunity for growth and transformation. This is exactly where I landed, God began to guide and show me how this experience of pain was propelling me to a life and purpose I could never imagine. To embrace and trust the process of growth I was invited into this season. I simply needed to decide to grow and transform through the pain. He knows the plans he has for me, plans to prosper me and not to harm me, one of a future and hope. (Jeremiah 29:11) To embrace the pain, you need to shift your perspective and see the pain as a teacher rather than an enemy. This means being open to learning from the pain and accepting the lessons that come with it. Embracing the pain requires a mindset shift, which could take time to achieve. However, when you embrace the pain, you begin to see it as a steppingstone towards a purpose-driven life.

Step Four: Reframe the Pain. The next step in transforming my pain to purpose was to reframe the pain. Reframing means looking at the pain from a different angle and finding meaning in it. When we reframe the pain, we change our perception of it and see it in a positive light. This was pivotal because I was able to see that cancer was not a death but a life sentence. That my husband leaving was a blessing in disguise, it propelled me rather the leaving me stuck. The pain awakened me from being a "walking dead person." To feel again and realize that I do have great purpose in this earth, one to grow leaders, one to speak on stages and share my real-life experiences in a vulnerable and transparent way. That there was no shame in my pain, my past or what I was "growing" through.

Tip: to reframe the pain, ask yourself questions such as; what have I learned from this pain? How has this pain helped me grow? What positive outcome has come from this pain?

Reframing the pain requires you to focus on the positive aspects of the pain and find meaning in it. This can help you move forward and find your purpose.

Step Five: Identify Your Values. Identifying your values is a crucial step in transforming pain to purpose and anchoring on your truth, faith, and purpose. Values are the principles or standards that guide your life. Your values can help you find your purpose and give meaning to your life. They serve as a compass to navigate life's challenges. I decided, as I wrote that chapter that launched me as an author, that I would honor my values and decide on my top five or six values which would anchor my decision-making process. The top values were Respect, Integrity, Generosity, Honesty and Humility, Trust, and Servitude. Any decisions I made in the future had to align with these values to get my YES.

TIP: To identify your values, ask yourself what's important to you? What do you stand for? What gives meaning to your life? When you know your values, you can align your life with them and find your purpose.

Step Six: Find Your Passion. Finding your passion is the next step in transforming pain to purpose. Passion is the driving force that motivates you to take action towards your purpose. When you find your passion, you will feel a sense of fulfillment and joy in what you do. This pain drove me to my passion and purpose, one of helping people grow to their highest potential. Our evolution should never stop. I found passion in writing, coaching, training, and helping people and organizations create and live their best life.

TIP: To find your passion, ask yourself what you love doing? What excites you? What would you do even if you weren't paid for it? When you find your passion, you can use it as a fuel to pursue your purpose.

Step Seven: Take Action. The last step in transforming pain to purpose is taking action. Taking action means putting your purpose into practice and making a difference in the world. When you take action towards your purpose, you are fulfilling your potential and living a meaningful life. As I reflect on the pain, I realize that I could not be where I am today, passed the pain, healed, and thriving in and on purpose without taking action. As I was invited to embrace and trust the process, it required taking steps. Some I didn't know where would lead me, taking steps forward despite the pain, and taking action towards living and leading in and on purpose. To take action, you need to have a plan and set goals. This can help you stay focused and motivated towards your purpose. Action can come in many forms such as volunteering, starting a business, or pursuing a new career. When you take action, you are not only transforming your pain but also making a positive impact on the world.

Transforming pain to purpose is a journey that requires commitment, honesty, determination, taking to heart God's Word. Having faith and trusting the process knowing that God is with you. John 16:33 is a reminder that during painful moments remember this "I have said these things to you, that in me you may have peace. In the world you will have tribulation. But take heart; I have overcome the world." I was reminded as I completed this chapter that in great pain one must find a secret place in which to dwell. A secret place where dwelling there required "next level "faith, submission, obedience, surrender, and humility." Without these, I could not trust God or His plans for me. Pain allowed me to make the life changing decision to anchor on my faith, truth (God's word), purpose (why I am here), and relentlessly trusting one of the most painful seasons in my life thus far.

I am aware that these are accounts I shared, and lessons learned are not the end of experiencing pain. I, however, now know where to go for truth and where to anchor my ship during future pain experiences…on God's Word, His truth, and His promises. No matter what presents, I must hold fast to my firm foundation. Pain is inevitable in life, and when dealt with, it can be transformed into a purpose-driven life. Into living a life in truth, forgiveness, peace, love, and joy. These seven steps on how to transform pain to purpose include acknowledging the pain, facing the pain, embracing the pain, reframing the pain, identifying your values, finding your passion, and taking action. When you follow these steps, you can transform your pain into a purpose-driven life and make a lifelong impact. Remember, there is power in deciding to anchor on your faith, on truth, and your purpose.

Ilka V. Wilson Biography

Ilka V. Wilson Vallee (formerly Ilka V. Chavez) Ilka is a fervent leader with an extensive track record for helping leaders of private and public entities, communities, and organizations reach their highest potential. She is the President of Corporate GOLD, a results-driven leadership consultant, strategist, certified life and emotional mastery coach, trainer, facilitator, and inspirational speaker. She has spent the last 35 plus years in various leadership roles honing her leadership, personal, and organizational transformation skills, and unique ability to work with others to improve work and life balance and improve quality and organizational performance. She has spoken on many stages nationally and internationally as well. Many speak of Ilka's stage engagement and motivational speaking as captivating and inspiring. Additionally, she is the #1 international bestseller author of ten books, four single-authored and 6 co-authored books. She is currently working on her book series, *What Leaders Say and Do*.

- Email: ilka@corporate-gold.com
- Website: http://www.corporate-gold.com/
- Facebook: www.facebook-com/ilkavchavez
- Instagram: www.instagram.com/chavezlka
- LinkedIn: linkedin.com/in/ILKA-chavez

Chapter 13:
When Life Hands You Lemons
By Dawn Kirk

I had just returned from an educator's convention in Chicago, feeling energized and excited about the upcoming school year. As a seasoned educator of 25 plus years, with a proven track record and stellar performance on my last evaluation as a department head, I was confident in my abilities as a professional to continue delivering excellence to my team and my students. However, life had other plans for me. Three weeks before I was scheduled to start my new teaching contract. I received an email that left me feeling numb. My new contract had been unexpectedly canceled due to budget cuts, leaving me with no job, a huge mortgage and other standing financial commitments including a car payment, and a small credit card debt. This new development like a sour lemon blindsided me from nowhere, leaving me with countless knots in my stomach. How was I to navigate this new development with strength and grace? Where was I going to secure another job on such short notice? At this point only God knew what my next step should be, and I counted on Him to reveal my next course of action without feeling unsure or insecure about fulfilling my obligations.

I had just four months left on my car payments and three and half years left to clear my mortgage. How would I cope? This turn of events was in no way a reflection on my abilities or likeability as a professional. It was just one of those opportunities to make lemonade from life's unexpected sour lemon experience. I was devastated, but I refused to be defeated. My faith in God would not allow me to wallow in despair. Like Job, I began to praise God in spite of these new circumstances, declaring that though I did not know the immediate future, I knew "WHO" holds the future. This was not by any means my first sour lemon experience, but it was by far the most intense and uncalculated. It would indeed be an incredible test of faith in God, resilience, and strength of character.

Initially, I was on autopilot as I knew I had to pivot, and against all odds find a new direction for my career. After much prayer, and a few dark moments of indecision, I decided to re-skill and start my own business. With my education background and project management training, I felt confident that I could turn my expertise into a profitable venture. There must be a way. I just had to find it! Although I was in uncharted territory, my experience in creating content frameworks and doing the research for those frameworks kicked into high gear. My first step was to do extensive research to find the right fit for my business project based on my expertise and the market need. I worked long hours with little rest, pouring over industry trends, and exploring different business models. It was a daunting task, but I was determined to make it work.

Time was not on my side. I also chose to align myself with a reputable company to build credibility fast and strategically. Just as I was getting my new business off the ground, I was hit with another challenge. I contracted Bell's Palsy, a condition that left half of my face paralyzed. What seemed like a regular day of business building, with an early morning call to one of my siblings in the UK, ended with me being admitted to emergency with the thought that I was experiencing a mild stroke. Luckily for me, I learnt from a medical expert years ago about the health benefits of taking cayenne pepper, and immediately following the facial distortions I observed in the mirror while speaking with my sibling, I began taking massive doses until a friend of mine took me to the hospital. I was admitted to a private room after being triaged and confirmed by the emergency physician that I did not suffer a stroke.

It seemed like I was constantly given snacks to eat to exercise my facial muscles. And I stayed there for two nights and a day before being released. It was a difficult time, I had to take a step back from my business building efforts to focus on my health. I was more intentional about resting, eating on time, being positive despite the challenges, and placing a greater focus on talking to God about how good it was to be alive. I was determined to embody my new mantra "it's not how you start your journey that counts…but how you finish." I claimed Jeremiah 29:11 which reminded me that God always has a plan and kept pressing on.

During my recovery and healing, I decided to learn a new skill that would help me take my business to the next level. I decided to learn how to build funnels, a skillset needed to help me automate my marketing and sales processes. I also dipped into my meager savings to pay my new mentor to teach me the art of funnel building. It was a steep learning curve, but I persevered. It turned out to be one of the best decisions I ever made. As I continued to grow in my business building efforts, I realized that I needed to expand my knowledge and skillset even further. I became a certified leadership coach and trainer, and then a certified digital marketer and consultant. These certifications gave me the tools I needed to help other educators succeed in their own businesses. With my newfound knowledge and expertise, I started a digital marketing agency for education entrepreneurs with a leadership training component. It was a challenging yet rewarding experience, and it allowed me to use my skills to help other educators achieve their own dreams of entrepreneurship.

Five years later, I am once again actively involved in training Generation Zs, but this time, I am doing it on my own terms. My business is growing beyond my wildest dreams, through providing keynote talks and training experiences for educators in North America, the Caribbean, and Africa. I've built a team of capable strategists for my club on Clubhouse, and I've broadened my horizons by meeting leaders in my industry from all around the world. Looking back, I never could have imagined that losing my job would lead me down this path. But when life handed me lemons, I refused to be defeated. Instead, I turned adversity into opportunity, and I never looked back. Life is full of unexpected twists and turns, and sometimes it can feel like the universe is conspiring against us. But when we're faced with adversity, we have a choice, we can either give up and let life defeat us, or we can rise up and meet the challenges head on.

Despite the setbacks, I refused to let defeat overtake me. Instead, I decided to pivot and start my own business, using my project management skills and teaching experience to build a career as an entrepreneur. And while it wasn't easy, it was one of the best decisions I ever made. So, how did I do it? How did I turn a devastating setback into a new opportunity? Here are some key lessons I learned along the way: 1. Don't be afraid to take risks. Starting a new business is a risky proposition, especially when you're doing it from scratch. Sometimes, taking risks is necessary if you want to achieve great things in life. When I decided to start my own business, I knew that it was a risk. I had no guarantees that it would be successful, and I had to invest a lot of time and a portion of my savings to get it off the ground. But I also knew that if I didn't take the risk, I would always wonder, "What if?" In the end, the risk paid off. My business has been successful, and I've been able to build a career that I love.

2. Keep pushing yourself. When you're starting a new business, there's always a lot of work to be done. You have to market yourself, build a client base, and manage all of the day-to-day tasks that come with running a business. It can be exhausting, and there were times when I felt like I was on the verge of burning out. With the strength that came from our Creator I was motivated to be resilient and keep pushing myself, and though I did not have all the answers I learned that I was capable of much more than I ever thought possible. No matter what your goals are, it's important to keep pushing yourself. Don't settle for mediocrity - strive for excellence, and never stop working to improve yourself.

3. Embrace change. One of the most important lessons I learned during my journey was the importance of embracing change. Life is unpredictable, and sometimes things don't go the way we planned. When my teaching contract was canceled, I could have easily fallen into despair. But instead, I chose to see it as an opportunity to try something new. I embraced the change, and it led me down a path that I never could have predicted. Don't be afraid of change - embrace it and see where it takes you. Sometimes the most unexpected opportunities can lead to the greatest rewards.

4. Believe in yourself. When you're faced with setbacks and challenges, it's easy to start doubting yourself. But the truth is, you are capable of achieving amazing things if you believe in yourself. During my journey, there were times when I felt like the odds were heavily stacked against me as the bills never stopped coming and my health remained a mountain to balance. Despite this, I was determined to succeed as an entrepreneur. I refused to let negative thoughts take hold. Instead, I focused on my strengths and reminded myself that with God I was capable of great things. Believe in yourself, and

don't let anyone else tell you that you can't achieve your dreams.

5. Keep learning. Another important lesson I learned was the importance of keeping an open mind to continued learning experiences. As an educator, I was used to being the one who taught, but as an entrepreneur, I quickly realized that there was so much I didn't know. I had to constantly learn new skills and strategies to stay ahead of the game. I became even more passionate about reading to succeed, invested in education and training, and read books and articles on business and marketing. I also acquired new mentors and reached out to other entrepreneurs and industry leaders to learn from their experiences. By constantly learning and expanding my knowledge, I was able to take action to stay ahead of the competition and grow my business.

6. Surround yourself with positivity. When you're faced with setbacks and challenges, it's important to surround yourself with positivity. Negativity can bring you down and make it harder to stay motivated and focused on your goals. Throughout my journey, I made a conscious effort to surround myself with positive people who believed in me and supported my dreams. I joined networking groups and attended conferences where I could connect with other entrepreneurs and like-minded individuals. By surrounding myself with positivity, I was able to stay motivated and inspired, even when things got tough.

7. Celebrate your successes. Finally, it's important to celebrate your successes, no matter how small they may seem. When you're starting a new business or working towards a big goal, it can be easy to get caught up in day-to-day struggles and forget to celebrate your accomplishments. But celebrating your successes is important for your mental health and

wellbeing. It reminds you that you're making progress and gives you the motivation to keep pushing forward. Throughout my journey, I made sure to celebrate every milestone, no matter how small. Whether it was landing a new client or hitting a revenue goal, I took the time to praise God, acknowledge my accomplishments, and give myself a tangible reward for my hard work.

In the end, my journey from educator to entrepreneur was a challenging but rewarding experience. By taking risks, pushing myself, embracing change, believing in myself, and continuing to learn, I was able to build a successful business and create a new career that I love. And if I can do it, so can you. No matter what setbacks you may face in life, remember that you have the power to rise up and meet your challenges head-on. With determination, hard work, and a positive attitude, you can achieve your dreams and create the life you've always wanted. As I reflect on my journey, I realize that ultimately, the key to my success has been first and foremost believing that God knew I would have to make lemonade from my lemons. I, therefore, embraced the willingness to adapt and pivot when faced with unexpected challenges. My experience taught me valuable lessons. It reminded me of the importance of self-care and the need to listen to my body. It also gave me a newfound appreciation for the resilience of the human spirit.

When my teaching contract was canceled, I could have easily given up and fallen into despair. Instead, I chose to take a leap of faith and pursue a new path as an entrepreneur. And while it wasn't easy, I was able to use my project management skills and teaching experience to build a successful business. I learned how to market myself, how to build funnels, and how to connect with clients in a digital world. But perhaps more importantly, I learned how to be resilient. I learned how to bounce back from setbacks, how to push through difficult times, and how to stay focused on my goals even when things felt overwhelming. While I can't say for sure what the future holds, I know that I'm ready for whatever comes next. Whether it's continuing to build my business, mentoring the next generation of education entrepreneurs, or simply enjoying the fruits of my labor, I'm excited to see where this journey takes me.

Because when life hands you lemons, it's not about what happens to you - it's about how you choose to respond. Today, I'm proud to say that under God I'm still going strong. My business has continued to grow, and I've expanded my reach and influence through digital channels like Clubhouse and other social media platforms. But perhaps the most rewarding part of my journey has been the connections I've made along the way. By reaching out to other education entrepreneurs, I've been able to build a supportive community of like-minded individuals who are passionate about making a difference in the world. And that, in the end, is what it's all about. When life hands you lemons, it's not about making lemonade for yourself - it's about sharing it with others and making the world a better place.

Dawn Kirk Biography

Dawn Kirk, known as Dawn Digital, is an educator, teacher, mentor, curriculum writer, leadership coach/trainer and digital marketing consultant with 30 plus years' experience. Her organization MMT Solutions helps Education Systems and Nonprofits in Africa, North America, and the Caribbean, build better brands using the 3 Es, a simple 3-step formula for success. Presently, she serves on the Atlantic Union Conference K-12 Curriculum Board and QUEST Bermuda Board of Governors. She is also curator of a Leadership Club on Clubhouse that promotes best practices in leadership. As a trainer for ETN Network Africa, Dawn empowers education leaders in West Africa to transform their organizations to build better brands. Professionally, she is Cornell University certified in Project Leadership and Systems Design, Maxwell Leadership certified as an Independent Executive Director, Amen University certified as a Brain-based trainer, and Billy Gene is Marketing Inc. certified as a Digital Marketing Consultant.

- Email: dkirk@marketmytrainingsolutions.com
- Website: https:/marketmytraininginstitute.com
- LinkedIn: www.linkedin.com/in/dawn-kirk-training/

Chapter 14:
Living Beyond Loss: Embracing Resilience and Finding Purpose
By Nicky Cuesta

My brother, Milton Cuesta, was born on January 8, 1981, a day that would forever be remembered because he shared the same birthdate with my mom's biggest idol, Elvis Presley. It would have been a twist of fate to name him Elvis. Due to my mother's intense birthing pain clouding her judgment, she ended up naming him Milton after our biological dad. Milton was the first grandson among ten on my mother's side, and he held a special place in my grandmother's heart. It was evident to everyone that he was her favorite. With his beautiful hazel glass eyes, bald head, and captivating smile, he had a natural charm that would capture the hearts of many. As the only child at the time, my mother was determined to cherish and raise him until he was five before even considering having another child. Little did she know that fate had already set another path for her. Five months later, my mother discovered that she was pregnant again—with me. Despite the initial shock, she embraced the idea of having another child and saw it as a blessing.

Her pregnancy progressed smoothly, and though she had no idea of my gender, she had a gut feeling that I was going to be a girl. It was an instinct that would prove to be right. In those days, gender reveals weren't a common practice, so the anticipation of my arrival was accompanied by excitement and uncertainty. My mother, fueled by hope and love, prepared for my arrival, creating a warm and welcoming space for her second child. But life has a way of challenging our plans, and tragedy struck just when everything seemed to be falling into place. Winters in Chicago were known for their freezing temperatures, and keeping warm was a constant struggle. Frozen heaters were a prevalent issue during the December through February months.

On one unfortunate day, someone thought it would be a good idea to defrost the boilers by using a huge aluminum drum filled with paper. What followed was a devastating three-alarm fire that engulfed my mother's apartment and everything she had built for us. The fire spread rapidly, and the only thing on my mother's mind was the safety of her son and unborn child. Ignoring the below zero temperatures, she ran barefoot to my grandmother's house, carrying Milton in her arms. It was a harrowing experience, and the fear she felt for her children was immeasurable. She lost everything in that fire, but the love and determination to protect her family remained unscathed. Other than that horrific experience, my mother's pregnancy was relatively uneventful until she went into labor with me. My grandmother playfully warned her not to call her if she had another boy. On the other hand, my stepdad confidently proclaimed that she would indeed have another boy. However, my mother had no doubt in her heart that she was carrying a girl, a little girl who seemed to be a bit stubborn even before entering the world.

My arrival was a bit more complicated than expected. The umbilical cord had wrapped around my neck, creating a distressing situation during labor. It was a difficult and nerve-wracking experience for my mother, but she pushed through with courage and was determined to give birth to me safely. Finally, on March 25, 1982, I entered the world, and to her immense joy, I was indeed the girl she had hoped for. My mother knew she would no longer seek to have any more children. As Milton and I grew older people often mistook us for twins due to our strong resemblance and the close emotional connection we shared. Wherever one of us went, the other was sure to follow. We attended the same schools, joined the same camps, and enjoyed family vacations together. Inseparable throughout the years. However, like any siblinghood, there was always a hint of rivalry between us. We constantly contended for our parents' attention and approval, seeking recognition for the choices we made in our lives.

It wasn't always easy being the younger sister, especially when societal norms seemed to boys. He was allowed more freedom and independence, which often left me feeling left behind and overshadowed. Our first major loss came when we were just thirteen and twelve years old. It was the passing of my grandmother, the very woman who had cherished and spoiled Milton among all the grandchildren. Her death was not just a loss for our family but a devastating blow to Milton, who had lost his guardian angel and one of the most influential figures in his life. The pain was indescribable, and the void she left behind was a constant ache in our hearts. As we started transitioning into our teenage years, our paths began to diverge.

While I started exploring the world of dating and parties, Milton remained steadfast in his disapproval of smoking and drinking. He had always been responsible and disciplined. As we both turned legal age, we faced another significant moment in our lives—we came out to our family and friends on separate occasions. It was a deeply personal and challenging process for each of us. Milton faced a bit more difficulty in getting everyone to embrace and accept him for who he truly was. There were individuals with reservations and judgments, but for the most part, people loved him for his happy-go-lucky spirit and looked beyond labels to see the person he was inside. Life took another unexpected turn when our parents decided to move to Philadelphia in 2000 during my senior year in high school. Milton and I found ourselves at a crossroads.

While I eventually chose to follow them to Philly, Milton remained behind to carve his own path. The distance between us was difficult, but our emotional connection remained strong. We kept in touch, calling each other regularly, and finding ways to share our lives from afar. A couple of years later in 2002, we found out that our adopted dad, the man who had given us his last name and shown us unwavering love and support, succumbed to liver disease due to his battle with alcoholism. His passing was a devastating blow to Milton and me, and it hit Milton especially hard. He was left to handle all the arrangements on his own, as I was in Philadelphia. I did fly back to Chicago to pay my respects. To my surprise, I was made aware that Milton had begun experimenting with drugs and was just not the same Milton that I knew. His choices worried and pained me, but my attempts to steer him back onto a healthier path were met with resistance.

We were becoming night and day when it came to our social lives and life choices seemed to be on separate paths. Years passed, and life brought both joy and sorrow. We celebrated milestones and achievements, but the shadows of addiction loomed over our lives. It was during this time that I received a call that would start changing everything. My mom phoned me with a sense of urgency in her voice. She explained that Milton had gotten himself into serious trouble and had landed in jail. My heart sank, knowing that he needed help and support more than ever. Addiction had taken its toll on him, and he was a mere shadow of the vibrant person I had known him to be. He fell deeper into drug use, which eventually led to heroin, and the grip of addiction tightened around him. We watched helplessly as he became entangled in a lifestyle we never could have imagined for him.

My mother and I made it our mission to help him overcome his addiction and find a path towards healing. We pleaded with him to move to Philadelphia, where we believed he could find a fresh start and a supportive environment. We hoped that being closer to us would provide the necessary distraction from the temptations that surrounded him in Chicago. With great difficulty, Milton agreed to come to Philadelphia after his release from jail in 2015. It was a bittersweet moment to have him back in our lives physically, but we knew that the battle against addiction was far from over. His struggles continued, and the cycle of relapse and recovery became all too familiar. Over the years, Milton faced numerous challenges, and his addiction led him back to jail multiple times. Each time he was released, we hoped for his redemption, but it proved elusive. Our family became familiar with the cycle of hope and heartbreak, and it took an emotional toll on all of us.

Despite the difficulties, I continued to believe in my brother's potential to overcome his addiction. We shared moments of joy and laughter amidst the hardships, and I cherished every one of those precious moments. There were days when he would seem like his old self again, and I would allow myself to hope that he had finally turned a corner. One sunny morning, just after his release from his last time in jail, we had a particularly wonderful day together. We went to the gym, listened to our favorite music, and laughed like we used to when we were kids. He seemed genuinely happy, and I could see a glimmer of the brother I had grown up with. It was a day filled with hope, and I allowed myself to believe that this time would be different.

After a day of sibling shenanigans, I dropped him off at my mom's, saying our goodbyes with smiles on our faces. Little did I know that it would be the last time I'd see him alive. Just 45 minutes later, the phone call came—the one that shattered my world and changed my life forever. My mother's voice was trembling as she told me that Milton wasn't breathing. Panic washed over me, and I rushed to her home as fast as I could. I ran upstairs to his room, my heart pounding in my chest, praying that it wasn't true. But as soon as I saw him lying there, non-responsive and cold, my world collapsed around me. The pain was unbearable, and I felt like I was living in a nightmare from which I couldn't wake up. My brother was gone—taken away by a merciless enemy we couldn't defeat. He died of an accidental overdose to heroin laced with fentanyl.

Addiction had claimed him, leaving a void in our lives that would never be filled. The grief was suffocating, and I felt a mix of emotions—anger, sorrow, and an overwhelming sense of loss. In the days that followed, our family rallied together, supporting one another through grief and pain. But the void left by my brother's absence was immense. I couldn't help but replay the moments we had shared, the laughter and the tears, and the hope we had held onto for so long. The replay of that final vision of his life taken too soon at the age of thirty-seven. Guilt washed over me as I questioned whether there was more I could have done to save him. I had tried so hard to be there for him, to offer support and love, but addiction had proven to be a formidable opponent. It was a battle he fought fiercely within himself, and ultimately, it was one he couldn't win.

I mourned the brother I had lost and grappled with the cruel reality that addiction had claimed yet another life. It felt unfair and unjust, and I couldn't comprehend why someone as kind-hearted and loving as my brother had to suffer such a fate.

During my grief, I tried to hold onto the memories—the good times, the laughter, and the love we had shared. I clung to the hope that he had found peace, free from the shackles of addiction that had plagued him for so long. That he no longer had to choose between his family or his vices. My brother's passing served as a poignant reminder of the devastating impact of addiction on individuals and families alike. It prompted me to advocate for greater awareness and support for those struggling with addiction and mental health issues. I knew that I couldn't bring my brother back, but I wanted his memory to be a catalyst for change—a beacon of hope for others facing similar battles.

In his absence, I vowed to live a life of purpose and meaning. Though my brother was no longer physically present, his spirit lived on within me and the countless lives he had touched. His story served as a reminder of the fragility of life and the importance of showing compassion and understanding to those facing their own battles. Milton Cuesta may no longer be physically present in this world, but his impact on my life and the lives of those he touched continues to resonate. I found solace in the belief that he was finally at peace, free from the chains of addiction that had held him captive for so long. His memory served as a constant reminder that life is fragile, and that we must cherish every moment with our loved ones, for we never know what the future holds. One of the most meaningful ways I can honor my brother's memory is by sharing his story and connecting with those fighting to overcome their demons.

On the flip side, my other passion is to serve those who are left on the other side of these unexpected encounters. The ones that are left behind to grieve these losses. I offer a listening ear, a hand to hold, and the reassurance that they are not alone on their journey. As I continue my journey of living beyond loss, I have learned to embrace resilience and find purpose in every step I take. My brother, Milton Cuesta, may no longer walk beside me, but his spirit remains a guiding light, urging me to seize each day with gratitude and determination. I have come to understand that life is too short to be wasted on regrets and what-ifs. Instead, I choose to live boldly, cherishing every moment, and using my experiences to support others facing their own trials. Through the pain and grief, I have discovered a newfound purpose in serving those left behind by addiction, offering compassion and understanding to their journeys of healing. As I honor my brother's memory, I find solace in knowing that by embracing life's challenges with an open heart, I can truly find purpose in the face of loss.

Nicky Cuesta Biography

Nicky Cuesta defies expectations, leaving an indelible mark as a mother, wife, and professional. Over two decades in corporate America, she shattered the glass ceiling in 2020 as she embraced her true purpose. Taking a leap of faith, Nicky igniting her own path to success. Nicky founded BALM GLOBAL, a transformative organization dedicated to nurturing leaders worldwide. As an award-winning speaker, author, and coach, she captivates audiences with her inspiring Podcast "Building a Leadership Mindset," amplifying the voices of revolutionary community leaders. As a Community Leader Nicky empowers members through life's challenges. Her upcoming initiative, EMPOWER TO INSPIRE, embarks on a nationwide tour across all 50 states starting January 2024, delivering her empowering message. With an unwavering mission to Build Leaders Globally, Nicky's passion is dedicated to transforming lives, to embrace potential and create positive change. Her remarkable journey exemplifies the power of faith, resilience, and living with purpose.

- Email: buildingaleadershipmindset@gmail.com
- Website: http://buildingaleadershipmindset.com/
- LinkedIn: https://linktr.ee/nickycuesta

CHAPTER 15:
Finding Life After Death
By Dr. Maureen McIntosh-Alberts

My life took a drastic turn on March 6, 2008, at 11:30 am, when I heard a knock on my front door. It was a visit I never expected, and the news that followed shattered my world. My husband, who had dedicated sixteen years of his life to improving the lives of orphans and vulnerable youths in Africa, had lost his own life in a tragic car accident in Tanzania. The sudden loss of my beloved husband, who had vowed to grow old with me, was devastating.

This was not the first time I had faced heartbreak in my life. I had been through two painful divorces. But this loss was different. The pain was so intense that I felt like a part of me had died inside. I knew that if I gave in to the grief, I could quite possibly die as well. But I consider myself a woman of great faith, and I believe everything that happens in our lives is directed by God. As one of my favorite scriptures says, "The steps of the righteous are ordered by the Lord." So, I turned to my faith to find a way to move forward.

From a young age, my grandmother raised me in the Catholic faith. She taught me to put all of my confidence in God, no matter what challenges or adversities came my way. But then, at the age of fifteen, I had a heart transformation experience after a missionary challenged my Catholic upbringing. He convinced me that there is only one mediator between God and man, and that mediator was Christ Jesus. He also convinced me that it was critical to trust Jesus for my salvation, so I willingly committed my life to Jesus Christ.

From that moment on, I embarked on a journey to understand the benefits that came with this salvation plan by studying the Bible. I learned that one of the many benefits is living a spirit-filled life. This spirit-filled empowered life comes from prayer, fasting, studying the Word of God, giving, and tithing. So, I committed myself to intentionally practicing these principles.

As I practiced these principles, my hunger and thirst for knowing God grew even stronger. My intimacy with God grew deeper in my prayer time. Over time, I learned how to bring every life experience to Him in prayer. It didn't matter what the experience was - small, large, good, or bad - I brought it to the Lord in prayer. I cherished that relationship with God so much that I couldn't envision living my life without spending time with Him in prayer day and night.

Growing up in the Caribbean, many children, in my environment at least, didn't have the privilege of having the love and guidance of their biological parents. I was one of those children. Being a single mom, my mom didn't have the resources to take care of me. So, she was forced to leave me in the care of her mom, my grandmother.

As a young child, longing for the love and attention of my parents, my grandmother didn't want me to idolize her. Instead, she imparted the wisdom of prayer and relying on God for all my needs. "God is your Father," she assured me. "Pray to Him, tell Him what you need. Don't be afraid to ask Him. He hears you, and He will provide." I wholeheartedly believed her.

A devout Roman Catholic, she shared with me her own journey of growing up without the love and guidance of her parents. Life had been extraordinarily difficult and filled with challenges for her, but she overcame them through faith in God. Her painful stories of abuse and neglect resonated deeply within me, etching themselves into the very core of my being. To this day, I carry those stories with me as a reminder to never give up when faced with life's adversities.

The most precious gift and the most valuable legacy my grandmother left me was her unwavering faith. It became the guiding light in my life. From childhood to the present, whenever I need help, no matter the nature of my need, instead of turning to friends or family first, I find solace on my knees in prayer. And without fail, every time I pray, I experience the divine peace, goodness, unconditional love, and provision of God. I shudder to think what my life would have been like had I not been raised to run to God in every situation.

It was this unwavering faith that sustained me when I received the devastating news of my husband's tragic death. I excused myself from the visitors, and gathering my son, daughter-in-law, and grandson, I hurried to my prayer closet—a sacred space in my home dedicated to communing with God. There, on my knees, I unleashed the torrent of pain and grief that consumed my heart. Tears streamed down my face as I cried out to God, my voice trembling with anguish.

"Oh Jesus, oh Jesus, oh Jesus," I sobbed. "Help me. Strengthen me. Give me the endurance to bear this unbearable pain. Hold me together, O God. I beg you, do not let me be consumed by this agony. Take my life as a living sacrifice. Even in this pain, I want to bring you glory. Let this pain strengthen me, Lord. You have been my rock through the pain of two divorces, the death of my beloved grandmother, and the loss of my first grandchild. Please, do not abandon me now. I need you."

In the depths of my despair, as I cried out to God, I heard an inner voice—a voice I had come to recognize as the Holy Spirit—whispering, "Worship me." In that moment, an incredible surge of strength flowed from the crown of my head, straight into the depths of my broken heart. And so, I began to worship. I started to recall and articulate, almost effortlessly, the goodness God had shown me throughout my life. It was as if another person had taken over, uttering words of affirmation and praise from the depths of my being. The Holy Spirit had seized control, worshiping God on my behalf.

As I continued in prayer, gratitude welled up within me. Despite the tears cascading down my cheeks, I offered heartfelt thanks to God for the years I had shared with my husband, for the blessings we had experienced as a couple. The more I expressed my gratitude, the stronger I felt emotionally. It was in the depths of grief, I made a profound commitment. I confidently surrendered my life into His hands.

Empowered by that internal strength, peace, and resilience, I found the confidence to trust Him to take care of me. There, on my knees, I affirmed, "Though You slay me" — drawing inspiration from the words of Job — "yet I will trust You. I know that You are faithful, even in the face of tragedy." In that sacred moment, I made a solemn vow to live a life of faith and commitment to God for the remainder of my days. I drew inspiration from the story of Job and his unwavering trust in the midst of unimaginable loss.

And then, something remarkable happened. In the midst of my deepest grief, I experienced a tremendous surge of inner peace and strength. The gift of resilient faith enveloped me, assuring me that, despite the pain, God's empowering presence would carry me through. It was a special anointing, a fresh infilling of the Holy Spirit, empowering me to become all that God had destined me to be and to do, for the honor and glory of His name. This anointing marked a personal transformation, a divine strengthening that fortified me from within.

With that empowering presence of the Holy Spirit, I was now able to face the death of my husband with unwavering resolve and confidence. Though the pain was still raw, and the tears flowed freely, I experienced the unmistakable presence of God. Inner strength and peace enveloped me, allowing me to face my guests with unwavering resolve, despite the excruciating pain still coursing through my soul.

Armed with this newfound strength, I proceeded to plan my husband's funeral service in Tanzania, deliver a heartfelt eulogy at his funeral in the United States, and journey to the Netherlands to attend yet another memorial service surrounded by family and friends.

It is said that life challenges have the power to make us either bitter or better. Some succumb to bitterness, allowing their pain to poison their souls. But others, like myself, see life's adversities as transformative opportunities, opportunities to become better versions of ourselves and make a positive impact on the lives of others.

My husband's tragic death became the catalyst for the most significant transformation in my life. Through the pain, I discovered my life's purpose. I recognized that, if not for his passing, I would have never embarked on this journey of self-discovery. My husband's death not only brought immense pain but also gifted me with three precious treasures: resilience, hope, and renewal. Rather than succumbing to despair and asking, "Why, God?" I chose to ask, "What, God? What is Your divine purpose for my life?" And in that question, I found my answer. His passing propelled me toward a life of purpose.

In December 2009, I founded Zorba's Orphans Fund, a 501(c)(3) organization, as a tribute to my late husband. His friends affectionately called him Zorba, a Greek word that encapsulated his passion for life. He was deeply committed to improving the lives of vulnerable youths in Africa, and so, I named the organization in his honor. Zorba's Orphans Fund became a vehicle to continue his mission and extend our reach to orphaned and vulnerable youths in Latin America, the Caribbean, and the United States.

Our ultimate goal is to join the global movement to end ignorance and poverty, liberating women and young girls from oppression and the horrors of human trafficking. Over the years, Zorba's Orphans Fund has provided education to countless orphaned and vulnerable youths and rescued many young girls from the clutches of human trafficking in Kenya.

We remain steadfast in our commitment to providing these vulnerable populations with a world-class education, empowering them to negotiate their place in society with confidence. Through education, doors are opened, and opportunities abound for them to experience a life of courage, freedom, and fulfillment.

But the journey from pain to purpose didn't end with the establishment of Zorba's Orphans Fund. It continued to transform me, molding me into the best version of myself. In 2009, I also embarked on an organizational consulting and coaching practice, where I guide and mentor faith-based leaders, helping them embrace the transformative power of life's challenges. Through coaching and mentoring, these leaders are empowered to make a profound impact in the lives of others, while also enjoying the personal and financial freedom that comes with their contribution.

In my work with others who have experienced their own share of pain and loss, I have witnessed the resilience of the human spirit. I have seen individuals rise from the ashes, transformed by their experiences, and empowered to create positive change in their own lives and in the lives of others.

In the depths of my pain, I discovered life after death—a life that embraces the memories of my beloved husband, carries his legacy forward, and continues to make a difference in the lives of those who need it most. I am no longer defined by the tragedies that have befallen me but by the resilience, faith, and love that have emerged from them. I have found a deeper connection with God, a renewed sense of purpose, and a profound gratitude for each day that I am given. I am learning to embrace the complexities of life, knowing that even in the face of adversity, there is always hope.

Through my own journey of pain and loss, I have discovered the power of transformation. It is through the darkest nights of the soul that we are given the opportunity to rise, to grow, and to become more than we were before. It is in those moments of surrender that we are infused with a strength that surpasses our own limitations.

In the face of tragedy, I have found a renewed sense of resilience, hope, and purpose. I have come to understand that in the process of letting go, we create space for something new to emerge. When we release our grip on what was, we open ourselves up to the possibilities of what can be. It is in the surrender that we find true freedom, for it is in surrendering to God's plan that we discover a life far greater than we could have ever imagined.

The death of my beloved husband remains a constant reminder that life's trials can shape us, molding us into vessels of strength and compassion. I choose daily to embrace resilience over bitterness, to allow the pain to refine me rather than define me. His passing became the catalyst for my purpose, and through it, I continue to discover the fullness of life's potential. My husband's death, though heart-wrenching, has ultimately shaped me into the person I am today—a person driven by a deep desire to make a positive impact and to bring glory to God in everything I do.

As I continue on my journey, I am reminded that finding life after death is not limited to physical death alone. There are many forms of death that we experience throughout our lives - the death of dreams, the death of relationships, the death of hope. But just as physical death is not the end, these other forms of death can also be steppingstones to new beginnings. And so, I journey onward, grateful for the transformative power of pain, knowing that with God by my side, I can face any challenge and find life, beauty, and purpose on the other side of it all.

Finding life after death is not about erasing the pain or pretending it doesn't exist. It is about embracing pain, acknowledging its presence, and allowing it to shape us into better versions of ourselves. It is through the cracks in our hearts that the light of healing and wholeness can enter.

Finding life after death is not an endpoint but a continuous journey of growth and discovery. It is a reminder that our lives are not defined by the tragedies we face but by how we respond to them. We have the power to choose whether we will allow our pain to consume us or whether we will use it as fuel to propel us forward.

Life challenges will come, but I now face them with unwavering faith and trust in God's plan. I have learned that even in the midst of grief, there is a life waiting to be lived—a life filled with purpose, meaning, and the opportunity to touch the lives of others. In the face of adversity, we can rise. In the midst of pain, we can find purpose. And through unwavering faith, we can transform our lives and the lives of others.

So, to anyone who is navigating their own journey of pain and loss, I offer these words of encouragement: trust that there is life after death. Embrace the process of healing, knowing that it is through the brokenness that we find our true strength. Allow your pain to be a catalyst for growth and have faith that God will guide you through the darkness into a brighter tomorrow.

Remember, you are not alone in your journey. The same power that breathed life into the universe resides within you. Draw strength from the love and support of those around you and seek solace in the presence of a God who walks beside you every step of the way.

May you find peace, healing, and a renewed sense of purpose as you navigate the path of finding life after death.

Dr. Maureen McIntosh-Alberts Biography

Rev. Dr. Maureen McIntosh- Alberts is a Behavioral Scientist, Human and Organizational Development Systems Specialist, specializing in the Management of Change in Multicultural Organizations. She has lived, worked, and traveled extensively nationally and internationally for over 15 years, leading organizational change management interventions, coaching, mentoring, and training staff in diversity equity and inclusion. Founder and CEO of Zorbas Orphans Fund, a 501C3, a charitable organization in Alexandria VA., she empowers the minds of orphans and vulnerable youths for the future, freeing girls from the egregious practice of human trafficking. A Certified Leadership Coach, Diversity Equity and Inclusion Trainer, Author, Speaker, Trainer DISC Certified Personality Assessment Consultant, ICF Certified Leadership Coach, Ambassador and Executive Director for The John Maxwell Team, she also heads The International Center for Empowerment and Leadership now EPIC Transformational Coaching Academy.

- Email: drmaureencoaching@gmail.com
- Website: www.epictransformationalcoachingacademy.com
- Facebook: www.facebook.com/zorbas.orphansfund